*Marian Engel
and Her Works*

Marian Engel (1933–1985)

ELIZABETH BRADY

Biography

MARIAN RUTH (PASSMORE) ENGEL was born in Toronto on 24 May 1933 to Mary Elizabeth and Frederick Searle Passmore. Although she has described herself as "a kind of placeless person,"[1] in reality she is a person of many places who has permanent roots in none. Her father was a World War I pilot who became a trade-school, auto mechanics teacher; his itinerant employment during the depression and war years took the family to a succession of southwestern Ontario towns — Port Arthur, Brantford, Galt, Hamilton, and Sarnia. "Moving a lot," she once remarked, "of course, puts you at an angle to your circumstances."[2] Inheriting no privileges based on birth, Engel belonged to a class of people who stressed education, hard work, practicality, moral responsibility, and respectability as the true measures of one's place in society. Her family were "Orange-Irish, extremely conservative, long-livers, and church-goers with a tendency to belong to Temperance societies."[3] From them she learned the importance of self-discipline and application; her non-conformist irreverence for bourgeois social values is self-taught.

In a bittersweet reminiscence called "The Girl from Glat: Memories of a Town That's Been Wiped off the Map," she has written about the influential wartime years from age five to ten when her family lived in Galt, a town representative of the provincial environment that figures so prominently in her fiction: "Your home was your family, you went where it went. If it went to a strange, gritty place full of dour people and beautiful buildings, fine. But now I know that if there's iron in my soul, it came from Galt."[4] This vein of "iron" she traces back to the small community's acute consciousness of class, nationality, and religious affiliation. The town's overriding Puritanism — equally manifest in her own family — taught her "to pay for joy" ("The Girl from Glat," p. 6) and that "every choice was a moral choice."[5] She credits the work ethic for her rigorous writing habits, and the "bleak environment" for provoking her to use her imagination: "We had those big flat fields. . . . I guess the tendency is to people them in your head" (Gibson, p. 108). In a tone implying limited victory over the ancestral antagonist, she records her retrospective thoughts about her background: "I walk along Beverly [the street she lived on] with interest, but not nostalgia, and a feeling of relief. I am finally grown up. I have survived. . . . and if I can't run fast under trains any more I have five books to defend myself with" ("The Girl from Glat," p. 7).

From Sarnia Collegiate Institute and Technical School, Engel entered McMaster University — then a Baptist institution — graduating in 1955 with a B.A. in language studies. She went on to McGill University, receiving her Master's degree in Canadian literature in 1957; her thesis, "A Study of the English Canadian Novel since 1939," was supervised by Hugh MacLennan, who was then working on *The Watch That Ends the Night*. Her brief teaching career included posts as English lecturer at Montana State University in Missoula (1957–58) and as geography mistress at a private girls' school, The Study, in Westmount, Montreal (1958–60). A Rotary Foundation Fellowship then took her to the Université d'Aix-Marseille in Aix-en-Provence (1960–61), where she studied French literature. Following a year-long stint working as a translator of foreign credit reports in London, England, and her marriage in 1962 to Howard Engel, who was then a CBC freelance radio broadcaster, she moved to Cyprus. She taught for a year at St. John's School (RAF) in Nicosia.

She returned to Canada in 1964; from that time on, she was based in Toronto. One year later, in the midst of completing her fourth unpublished novel, Engel became the mother of twins, Charlotte and William. In the early 1970s, she broke with her housebound, domestic existence to begin a phase of active political work. She became the first chairperson of the Writers Union of Canada in 1973. Two years later, she was appointed a trustee of the Toronto Public Library Board. Of her three-year trusteeship, Engel observed: ". . . it taught me a very great deal about the workings of power structures and how social change is brought about."[6] She separated from her husband, who was by then a prominent CBC Radio producer, in 1975; they were divorced two years later. During this period, she also served as a member of the City of Toronto Book Prize Committee and of the Canadian Book and Periodical Development Council. In 1977 she moved to Edmonton as writer-in-residence at the University of Alberta; she stayed on for another year to teach creative writing. During 1980–81 Engel was the University of Toronto's fourteenth writer-in-residence.

Marian Engel died of cancer on 16 February 1985 at the age of fifty-one. Although the disease had been diagnosed six years earlier, she maintained an active life and continued to write — in spite of diminishing energy, frequent hospitalizations, and great pain.

Marian Engel began writing shortly after she learned the alphabet. Her first published article, "The Postman," appeared on 20 April 1947 in *The Canadian Girl*, a United Church Sunday-school paper, to which she became a regular contributor; over the next five years, she published twenty-five articles and nineteen poems in the paper.[7] Her first published short story, "A Summer's Tale," appeared in *Seventeen* (July 1952), winning honourable mention in the magazine's annual fiction contest; the following year, her story "Al" (Jan. 1953) won her third prize in the same contest. While still a high-school and university student, she worked as a reporter for *The Sarnia Observer*. At McMaster she belonged to the group that published the student newspaper (*Silhouette*; she served as associate editor), literary magazine (*The Muse*, which she edited), and yearbook. During her undergraduate years, her poetry and short stories appeared in *Silhouette* and *The Muse*.

What she calls her "apprentice work" (Gibson, p. 106) includes four novels — "stinkers that naturally weren't published."[8] The first, an "academic spoof" called "The Pink Sphinx," was written in 1958, when she was teaching at Montana State University, in collaboration with a friend, Leslie Armour, who provided the plot. While living in England, she wrote "Women Travelling Alone," a "big scrappy novel with time and everything out of perspective," a premature attempt to write the memoirs of a forty-year-old woman: it "had some lovely . . . pieces of writing, but it didn't hang together or know enough of time and space" (Gibson, p. 106). She collaborated on a "terrible" detective novel, "Death Comes for the YaYa" (Klein, p. 8), with her husband, who "made up the plot," while they were living in Cyprus: "I wrote it in order to get down a lot of information, a lot of sensations I wanted to keep" (Gibson, p. 106). Some of the material from this manuscript was later incorporated into her Cyprus novel, *Monodromos*. A fourth unpublished novel, "Lost Heir & Happy Families," was written during 1964–65.

Engel's *No Clouds of Glory* was published in 1968. Six more novels followed: *The Honeyman Festival* (1970); *Monodromos*(1973); *Joanne: The Last Days of a Modern Marriage* (1975); *Bear* (1976); *The Glassy Sea* (1978); and *Lunatic Villas* (1981). A collection of nineteen short stories, *Inside the Easter Egg*, appeared in 1975; a second collection, *The Tattooed Woman*, was published posthumously in 1985. She also wrote two children's books, *Adventure at Moon Bay Towers* (1974) and *My Name Is Not Odessa Yarker* (1977), and the text for a nonfiction "coffee table" book, *The Islands of Canada* (1981). At the time of her death, she left uncompleted an historical novel she had worked on intermittently for twelve years.

From 1968 until her death, she published numerous book reviews in leading Canadian and American newspapers (she was a regular contributor to *The Globe and Mail*'s book pages) and articles on a wide range of topics in magazines (*Chatelaine* was her biggest outlet), newspapers, professional journals, and books. From November 1981 through to September of 1982, she contributed a weekly column, entitled "Being Here," to *The Toronto Star*.

Engel was the recipient of three Canada Council senior arts fellowships (1968, 1973, 1976). In 1977 *Bear* won the Governor General's Award for the best English-language fiction of 1976. *The Glassy Sea* was awarded the 1978 Canadian Authors Association Silver Medal for Fiction. She travelled to Australia in March 1980 to participate as the Canadian representative in the biennial Adelaide Festival. In May 1980 she was awarded the 1979 McClelland and Stewart Award for fiction writing in a Canadian magazine for her short story "Father Instinct," published in *Chatelaine* (Aug. 1979). On 24 February 1982 she was awarded the City of Toronto Book Award (1981) for *Lunatic Villas* — a prize she shared with Claude Bissell, author of *The Young Vincent Massey*. Later that same year, she was appointed an Officer of the Order of Canada. In 1984 Marian Engel was named Metro Toronto YWCA's Woman of Distinction in Arts and Letters.

Tradition and Milieu

For Marian Engel, the world of ideas was a constant transgressor of national boundaries: the practice of writing novels — and literary criticism — in terms of national categories was as alien to her as would be the shelving of library books according to class, race, or gender. Her passionate commitment to an indigenous culture, to supporting a viable Canadian publishing industry, and to improving the economic lot of Canadian writers through her advocacy of such schemes as a public lending right and a pension scheme should not obscure the essential *cosmopolitanism* of her outlook. Her eclectic formal education, her five-year residency and many trips abroad, fluency in three languages, and her extensive reading and book reviewing all contributed to enlarging her perspective. She once called herself an "omnist" (Gibson, p. 103): she was a voracious reader of "good books" — whatever their writers' nationality.

It would be extremely misleading to isolate specific influences on her development as a writer or to place her within a sharply defined literary school or tradition. When asked by an interviewer, "Do you think that any writers have been influences on you?" she replied: "Oh, I think almost any writer I've ever read" (Gibson, pp. 102–03). In a more recent interview, however, she cited T. S. Eliot as "another big influence" and "generally the English mystics" as having appealed to her; Lawrence Durrell's *The Alexandria Quartet* "influenced [her] a lot" (Klein, pp. 20, 11). Her reluctance to restrict herself to a movement probably has its origins in her schooling in the 1940s and 1950s, when the study of literature was virtually synonymous with "British" and "American." In conversation and in writing, she ranged with confidence over the entire history of the English novel from Aphra Behn to the latest Beryl Bainbridge; among her twentieth-century favourites were Virginia Woolf, Elizabeth Bowen, Doris Lessing, Iris Murdoch, and Margaret Drabble. She was also well versed in French fiction, particularly those writers who are preoccupied with its more innovative technical aspects — Balzac, Flaubert, Proust, Gide, George Sand, Colette, Camus, Françoise Sagan, Michel Butor, and Michel Tournier. Among the Latin and South American writers, she centred out Jorge Luis Borges, Gabriel García Márquez, and Julio Cortázar. Such diverse novelists as South African Nadine Gordimer, Australians Christina Stead and Patrick White, Japanese Yukio Mishima, and Italian Italo Calvino she highly regarded. Engel did not read much American literature, and she was never a keen poetry reader. Once, when asked if she was "interested in critical theories of literature," she replied: "Well, I'm way behind. I can understand the Levi-Strauss sort of stuff, but some of the other new critics don't make sense to me. Many critical theories have more to do with analyzing texts than with *constructing* them. Sure, they're good for deconstructing, but I don't think I want to spend my life constructing texts for people to deconstruct."[9]

One can isolate, however, two strongly linked aspects of her identity as a writer. She is a *Canadian* writer, who was given to remarking that "the American experience is not ours" (Cowan, p. 8). Because she saw writing fiction as, "in a serious emotional sense, writing social history,"[10] she defined as one of the novel's primary functions the recreation of a felt sense of place — in her case the Canadian landscape. Related to her concept of fictional place was her awareness of the effect of being a *woman* writer: "It affects my writing because a part of my particular regionalism . . . is my gender . . . . [W]omen's experiences are a different place" (van Herk and Palting, p. 40).

Although Engel could remark with satisfaction that, in the modern Canadian novel, "place and reality [i.e., the 'real lives we lead now'] have come together and, in women's work, extraordinarily" ("The Woman as Storyteller," p. 6), prior to this happy convergence, Canadian fiction took a sluggish course. During her adolescence, there was very little to nourish the aspiring young writer in search of models in the domestic tradition. What was available was clearly antipathetic both to Engel's earthy sensibility and to her own literary ambitions. The genteel tradition typified in the nineteenth century by the work of Anna Jameson, Susanna Moodie, and Catharine Parr Traill and in the early part of this century by the romances of Lucy Maud Montgomery, Mazo de la Roche, and Marian Keith exemplified the saccharine aridity into which women writers fell when their "real lives" were "confined" or "taboo." The genteel novel was a mere confection, "tarted up with primroses and ersatz passion" ("The Woman as Storyteller," p. 6). There can have been little in that repressive tradition, uncomfortably reminiscent of Engel's Puritan heritage, to inspire the woman who eventually was to create a heroine who makes love to a bear. Although she carried her persistent interest in Canadian fiction over into her M.A. thesis on the Canadian novel from 1920 to 1955 (although entitled "A Study of the English Canadian Novel since 1939"), these were not watershed years: the period scarcely saw the establishment of a "major" tradition. What did count was the transition from romance to representational realism. Her academic survey includes such notable works as Robert Stead's *Grain* (1926); Morley Callaghan's *Such Is My Beloved*

(1934), *They Shall Inherit the Earth* (1935), and *More Joy in Heaven* (1937); Irene Baird's *Waste Heritage* (1939); Sinclair Ross's *As for Me and My House* (1941); Hugh MacLennan's *Barometer Rising* (1941) and *Two Solitudes* (1945); Frederick Philip Grove's *The Master of the Mill* (1944); Edward McCourt's *Music at the Close* (1947); W. O. Mitchell's *Who Has Seen the Wind* (1947); Ethel Wilson's *Hetty Dorval* (1947) and *Swamp Angel* (1954); Hugh Garner's *Cabbage-town* (1950); and Ernest Buckler's *The Mountain and the Valley* (1952). But her study ends with the Callaghan-Garner-MacLennan generation — at the very point in time when an important new phase in Canadian fiction was emerging, the future direction of which was foreshadowed by the publication in 1959 of Sheila Watson's *The Double Hook* and Mordecai Richler's *The Apprenticeship of Duddy Kravitz*. This was also the time when Engel wrote her first (unpublished) novel.

In Engel's view, the publication of Gabrielle Roy's first novel, *The Tin Flute* (1945), signalled a turning point in women's fiction from the work of "lady novelists" to that of "serious women writers." "It was Gabrielle Roy who first brought that life my mother's generation called 'sordid' to women's writing in Canada. *The Tin Flute* was a body-blow to the genteel tradition" ("The Woman as Storyteller," p. 7). It was, however, Engel's own contemporaries (mostly women) who were to produce the body of work she most admired. Prior to "the great bulge of creativity" in this country that began in the late 1960s, she "never felt influenced by writers in this country" (Klein, pp. 11, 10).

She commented in the early 1970s that, while ". . . it matters that there should be an intellectual community . . . ," she found it difficult to know other writers because ". . . there's very little shop to talk, except agents" (Gibson, p. 94). Her subsequent involvement with the Writers Union created the requisite shop-talk; from 1973 on, she actively served as a speaker and writer on behalf of the community, participating regularly in panel discussions, conferences, public readings, and interviews. It was not uncommon for Engel to turn ostensibly self-promotional events into disinterested pleas for reforming the financial status of her fellow writers. She contributed significantly to raising public awareness of such issues as copyright and public lending right, and of the specific problems confronting the woman writer whose family responsibilities often conflict with her career.

Her union involvement gave her lively contact with numerous Canadian writers, several of whom were subsequently among her closest friends — especially Adele Wiseman and Margaret Laurence. Other good friends in the literary community include Margaret Atwood, Timothy Findley, Graeme Gibson, Gwendolyn MacEwen, Judith Merril, Jane Rule, and David Lewis Stein. Laurence and Wiseman, along with Alice Munro, she once referred to as the "reigning triumvirate of English Canadian women writers" ("The Woman as Storyteller," p. 7). It is interesting to note that those writers she most esteemed, and to whose novels her own bear the closest affinities, are the writers of her own gender in whose work "place and reality" have strongly converged: she pointed with great respect to Laurence's small, prairie town of Manawaka, Wiseman's North Winnipeg Jewish community, and Munro's southwestern Ontario town, Jubilee. The defining attribute of her novels is their strongly marked regional character. Critical to the identity of her female protagonists is their retrospective sense of place; in their searches for a clearer comprehension of themselves, they obsessively track back to a sharply etched geographical matrix. The five small towns of Engel's peripatetic past coalesce into the quintessential image of rural Ontario during the harsh decades of the 1930s and 1940s.

Notwithstanding these affinities with her peers, any present attempt to definitively place her work in the contemporary context would be premature; starting with the 1968 publication of her first novel, Engel produced, on average, another book of fiction every eighteen months. She died in mid-career. Certainly it is too early to assess her influence on the younger generation of writers or on the international literary scene. Although five of her novels have been published in the United States, and two in England, her work does not command a large readership in either country.

One might predict, though, the general lines of a future critical placement. Her major themes — and the fact that her second and third novels and her first short-story collection appeared under the House of Anansi imprint — suggest a slot in the Canadian literary nationalism phase of the late 1960s through mid-1970s. Along with such early Anansi writers as Dennis Lee, Peter Such, Dave Godfrey, Margaret Atwood, Graeme Gibson, and Matt Cohen, Engel is concerned with a literary exploration of ancestral identity that concurrently embraces the personal and cultural implications of place. In addition to the three women writers discussed above, her work has certain affinities with that of male novelists Gibson, Cohen, and Rudy Wiebe. Her fictional settings, like theirs, often are peculiarly closed communities — mentally confined environments which derive their homogeneity from a repressive set of values, usually religious in nature, that is hostile to the young protagonist. The latter's aspirations for a wider life eventually bring him/her into contact with the often subversive values of a more catholic world. It is in the area of content, then, that Engel's novels resemble theirs; with respect to narrative structure and technique, she is less innovative and resourceful than her male counterparts.

It also seems likely that Engel's work eventually will be placed in the context of the "new wave" feminist fiction that first surfaced in the early 1970s. Here her place is more problematic because she is a transitional, rather than a vanguard, figure. Her typical heroines are conventional, well-educated, middle-class women whose searching preoccupations with male/female relationships, marriage, and motherhood speak strongly to the thousands of female — and sympathetic male — readers whose own lives are similarly preoccupied. But she will not, I think, be seen as a "breakthrough" writer in feminist fiction: she does not write from the more subversive viewpoints that inform radical feminist and overtly lesbian novels. Engel once observed that "I know I'm usually considered reasonably retrograde by the women's movement. I don't know whether there is such a thing as a free woman, or a free person, or whether, indeed, freedom is desirable" (Cowan, p. 8). That "freedom is desirable" is the one unnegotiable premise of contemporary feminism, and the fiction that underwrites this first principle is overtly political in content, reaching well beyond patriarchal validation and bourgeois value systems; it is frequently experimental in form. The radical implications of this "freedom" are adumbrated in the novels of such young English Canadian writers as Aritha van Herk (*Judith*, *The Tent Peg*, and *No Fixed Address*), Susan Musgrave (*The Charcoal Burners*), Joan Barfoot (*Abra*, *Dancing in the Dark*, and *Duet for Three*), Monica Holden-Lawrence (*Mad about the Crazy Lady*), and Sharon Riis (*The True Story of Ida Johnson*). They are vividly present in the work of Québécois writers Nicole Brossard, Madeleine Gagnon, Geneviève Amyot, Louky Bersianik, France Théoret, and Miréille Lanctôt, for whom the choice of a "feminine" subject inevitably has led to the exploration of various strategies of linguistic subversion and the attempt to create a "woman's discourse." Engel strongly disassociated herself from such experiments with language: "To a certain extent, you have to look at sexism as a historical and socio-logical accident; you can't start mucking up the English language in an attempt to redress that accident" (Corbeil, p. 3).

Critical Overview and Context

"My biggest complaint is that I often feel that my work is not taken seriously by the critics" (van Herk and Palting, p. 12). Speaking while she was still in the first decade of her literary career, Engel should not have been too irritated by her perception of critical neglect. Yet as late as 1981, she commented: "The only people who have done serious critical articles on me are Ann Hutchinson and George Woodcock. I'm not considered to be a post-modernist, so I'm O-U-T for many academics. They can't have read my books" (Matyas and Joiner, p. 5). Certainly one fact can not be overlooked: the publication of *Bear* resulted in the most sensational attention ever paid a single novel in the history of Canadian publishing. In the course of a few weeks, Engel shot from being a figure of minor inter-est on the literary scene — "I stopped being a small press writer" (Klein, p. 27) — to a position of considerable notoriety that extended well beyond the usual readership circles. Unfortunately the novel's "pornographic" content attracted a good deal of extra-literary attention. Both the perpetuation of this original interest and much of the subsequent reaction to it have had a distorting effect upon her reputation. She stands the risk of being known as a prolific "one book" novelist — and one who is too often praised or damned for reasons unrelated to her real achievement.

The one generalization that does hold about Engel's standing is that it remains uncertain. With the single, vexed exception of *Bear*, none of her fiction has commanded sufficient critical agreement to provide a consensus, either positive or negative. Roughly speaking, opinion is evenly divided as to the merits of the other novels. Even those literary reputations that appear to be secure are always subject to revaluation; the problem of assessing Engel's reputation is compounded by the slow progress to maturity of most Canadian lit-erary criticism. Too often, appraisals of her novels are contingent upon the reviewer's or critic's sense of accord with their ideas and implied values. Increasingly these ideas and values have been squeezed to fit into two narrow criteria: the degree to which a book is idiosyncratically "Canadian" (the Survival Theme); and the degree of its adherence to, or deflection from, feminist ideological "correctness" (the Liberated Heroine Theme). Neither thematic approach advances the exegetical and evaluative functions of literary criticism, and Engel's reputation remains in flux, pinned as it is to nothing more substantive than her reviewers' whims and impressions of the moment.

A bibliographical search of what has been written on Marian Engel uncovers over 150 reviews; more than three dozen biographical profiles; four in-depth interviews; and entries in the standard biographical and literary reference works. To date only seven scholarly articles devoted exclusively to her fiction have appeared; of these, six are largely descriptive and the seventh is pure invective. This survey begins with the 1968 reviews of *No Clouds of Glory.* Her first novel was generally judged to be deficient in the areas of structure and characterization. The "tautness" of the first half of the book was felt to be lost in a plethora of extraneous detail in the second,[11] and the time sequences were "inexpertly handled."[12] One reviewer praised the novel's skilful "interweaving" of Toronto and European settings,[13] while another complained that "the sense of place is never secure."[14] On the important subject of Engel's characterization of her narrator-protagonist, opinion was evenly divided between those who found the narrator's candor praiseworthy and those who felt her to be a tedious, overtalkative, self-pitying "shrew."[15] The thin depiction of minor (especially male) characters was noted.[16]

The reviewers' initial ambivalence about Engel's central character sharpened in the 1970 reviews of *The Honeyman Festival.* One writer disparagingly categorized it as "a woman's book," and pregnant Minn Burge as an everyday nagging housewife, the dramatization of whose inner life became so claustrophobic that she remains merely a "biological phenomenon."[17] Another declared that the novelist, through her creation of an exemplary liberated heroine, "has permanently joined the ranks of revolutionary women writers."[18] Two reviewers had complaints about style, which they variously described as the "arch telegraphic prose"[19] and the "irritating mannerisms"[20] of Engel's literary pretentiousness.

Monodromos drew criticisms similar to those of *No Clouds of Glory.* It, too, was found deficient in structure: ". . . the form of the novel is not only episodic; it is also fragmentary . . . . *Monodromos* does not emerge into a pattern."[21] Again it was generally observed that Engel had failed to fully and credibly characterize her protagonist, who never comes to life and who "remains a tourist — someone who doesn't penetrate the surfaces."[22] The novel received high praise for style, though, particularly as it serves to create a vivid sense of place: "The style is elliptical, a mosaic of bits of thought, voices, dreams, images . . . . [T]he texture is closely wrought, as packed with significance as poetry";[23] Engel "writes with great economy and with a kind of Rose Macaulay learning."[24] Two critics observed that the centrality of setting over character distinguished the book — but in an altogether different genre, that of the "travel guide."[25] On the other hand, a reviewer for *The Times Literary Supplement* found *Monodromos* an "over-researched, over-allusive novel" written "with a blend of self-regarding simplicity, pedantry and grandiloquence";[26] in a similar vein, another criticized the self-conscious cleverness and "fragmentary 'fine writing.'"[27]

At this point in the novelist's career, the book reviewers could not agree upon even the *number* of books she had written ("There can't be many fresher and less pretentious first novels,"[28] exclaimed one). However, her work was beginning to attract wider notice. She was included in Graeme Gibson's 1973 collection of interviews, *Eleven Canadian Novelists*, and received her first "academic" treatment in Frank Davey's *From There to Here: A Guide to English-Canadian Literature since 1960* (1974). Davey's negative estimation of her three novels did nothing to enhance her reputation. He viewed Engel's "problem" as a novelist (a dilemma shared by her heroines) as analogous to the "post-modern problem of finding meaning within chaos."[29]

The year 1975 marked the publication of two books: *Joanne*, her fourth novel, and a collection of nineteen short stories, *Inside the Easter Egg*. Neither book, however, represents mainstream Engel, and their critical reception put her reputation more or less on hold. *Joanne* was commonly judged to be "a slight book": ". . . one misses here that whole self-indulgent, elitist, and delicious play with allusions, word games, footnotes, and half-registered references from musty libraries that pepper the other novels."[30] Although a few reviewers discovered local felicities within some of the stories, on balance *Inside the Easter Egg* received lukewarm notices as "a patchy book"[31] that "doesn't greatly expand the range of Engel's considerable talents."[32] Ronald Labonte's criticisms of the stories are particularly serious ones because he regards them as equally applicable to Engel's novels, especially to *Bear*. He extends the central charge which several reviewers earlier had brought against her: "The problem rests squarely with Engel's refusal to create characters who live and act and respond in the complex fashion of real people . . . . Her themes titillate the reader but are never given close scrutiny; there is only a clever appearance of depth caused by the superficial resemblance of her characters and their traumas to ourselves."[33]

The first scholarly article exclusively devoted to one of Engel's novels, Douglas H. Parker's "'Memories of My Own Patterns': Levels of Reality in *The Honeyman Festival*," appeared in 1975. The critic examines "the film" as the recurring metaphor to depict the "inner struggle between past and present that Minn experiences."[34] Parker's painstaking compendium of the successive film references is primarily descriptive, and his interpretation of the metaphor's cumulative meanings is misleading.

The sudden turning point in Marian Engel's career was occasioned by the publication of *Bear* (1976). Shortly after its discreet hardcover appearance, word spread like a dirty rumour that it was a titillating, taboo-shattering book — as well as a small masterpiece. Of the more than fifty reviews I have tracked down, those that overwhelmingly praise *Bear* outnumber its detractors on a three-to-one ratio. Generally speaking, two aspects of the novel were singled out for distinction: the masterful cross-genre blending of realism and myth, and its singularly appropriate, spartan prose style. Adele Wiseman's illuminating remarks offer the best summation of this line of approach:

> It is a measure of the great skill with which this story is handled, that while adhering strictly to a simple and compelling story line, and never losing credibility on the naturalistic level, Ms. Engel manages to suggest such a wealth of allusive implication, on so many other levels. All the allusions work together to build an atmosphere of urgency and intensity, an atmosphere she nevertheless refuses to exploit by in any way artificially heightening her prose. Her writing retains its beautifully balanced and compellingly objective tone, though laced throughout with a kind of dry drollery.[35]

In an essay by Elspeth Cameron exploring its allegorical significance,

Bear received its scholarly honorific imprimatur in the *Journal of Canadian Fiction* the following year.[36] Quite another line of attack was pursued in a handful of far less influential reviews and articles, the focus of which was the offensiveness of the heroine's "obscene" relationship with the bear. This was a relatively muted objection, verbally couched in such admonitions as "it is a solemnly pretentious perversion of one of the oldest Romantic themes"[37] — until Scott Symons raised it to a frenetic pitch in his vitriolic essay "The Canadian Bestiary: Ongoing Literary Depravity," which originally appeared in the *West Coast Review*, was excerpted in *The Canadian Forum*, and became the topic for William French's book column in *The Globe and Mail*. Symons located the novel's "obscenity" in the national, class-bound scheme of things: ". . . the essential 'dirtiness' of this book . . . is *not* the sexing with that poor, bedraggled, tame and chained black bear . . . . What *is* dirty, finally obscene, about *Bear*, is the author's pretension . . . . *Her* pretension, and that correlative furtive (and cowardly) process of attacking and deriding the 'genteel Canadian tradition' she so desperately wants to rip off as, in part, her own. The obscenity in this last being the destruction of what you lusting want. Which is a cultural recipe for suicide."[38] Unlike the positive appraisals of *Bear*, Symons' blank refutation does not have the merit of inviting further elucidation and debate. It did give him fifteen-minute celebrity status in the normally polite world of Canadian letters.

A few years subsequent to the reviews that appeared at the time of its publication, three academic treatments of *Bear* were published; each is more concerned with explicating theme and symbol — particularly with a view to explaining away any alleged "pornographic" content — than with discussing and evaluating formal elements. In her 1979–80 essay "The Bearness of Bear," Margaret Gail Osachoff argues that ". . . what appears on the surface to be a modern romantic pastoral like *Lady Chatterley's Lover* . . . is really an inversion or ironic treatment of such myths," intended to warn against "romanticizing nature."[39] The novel is classified as a romance in Donald S. Hair's "Marian Engel's 'Bear'" (1982): ". . . we must say . . . that the conventional action of romance — the quest in search of treasure which is guarded by a monster — lies behind the action of this novel."[40] He elaborates the symbolic significance of the octagonal house ("wholeness" and "regeneration" [p. 36]) and the bear ("integration of body and mind" [p. 39]), in the process strenuously wringing meaning out of quite a few ordinary objects and actions that are inappropriately put to work in the service of his thesis. Finally, Michelle Gadpaille, in her 1982 "A Note on 'Bear'" — a rather pedantic exegetical piece — examines the outbuildings behind the octagonal house and Colonel Cary's cryptic bear-notes as representative of certain basic romantic dilemmas.[41]

In 1978 Ann Hutchinson offered the first extended retrospective survey of the oeuvre in "Marian Engel, Equilibriste." This mainly descriptive, thematic essay examines the special "difficulties of being a woman and an artist"[42] through a discussion of Engel's use of her own upbringing as material for her fiction and relates this autobiographical component to her heroines' ambivalent perceptions of their pasts.

Critical response to *The Glassy Sea* slipped back into the mixed-bag pattern that took shape around her earlier fiction prior to *Bear*, sounding echoes of the main lines of approach. Like *Monodromos* and *Bear*, it was widely praised for its style, particularly its vivid evocation of the western Ontario and convent settings — "the sharply observed circumstances of her upbringing and the sheer sensuous mass of the Christian monastic tradition."[43] Her unconvincing presentation of male characters and the protagonist's unduly restrictive viewpoint were noted, as was the case with *No Clouds of Glory* and *The Honeyman Festival*.[44] Several reviewers expressed dissatisfaction with plot and structure (specifically with pacing and plausibility), problems which earlier were felt to considerably weaken *Monodromos*.[45] One new criticism surfaced — that Engel has burdened the conclusion with a "surfeit of [feminist] rhetoric and polemic."[46] In spite of the overall assessment of *The Glassy Sea* as an "uneven" novel, the attention paid *Bear* permanently assured Engel a place as a writer whose work, far from being neglected, would be paid the serious attention it merits.

Indeed, Engel was included in Alan Twigg's 1981 collection of interviews, *For Openers: Conversations with Twenty-Four Canadian Writers*;[47] and in June 1984, the Vancouver feminist quarterly *Room of One's Own* published a special issue on Marian Engel, to which George Woodcock contributed an essay, "Casting Down Their Golden Crowns: Notes on *The Glassy Sea*."[48] After discussing the novel as "a remarkable meditation on faith, hope and charity and on the impossibility of being Mary if you are indeed Martha"(p. 46), he concludes with very high praise for the book: "*The Glassy Sea* is

Marian Engel's best novel up to the present" (p. 52); he identifies as "her prime virtue as a writer" her "prose style, with its excellent simplicity and perfect pitch" (p. 53).

Reviews of *Lunatic Villas* are consistent only in their inconsistency of appraisal, with the balance tipped slightly in favour. The reviewers seem more or less agreed upon just two aspects of Engel's single foray into the comic novel. However variable her performance in other elements of craft, her assurance as a prose stylist of very high calibre persists.[49] But even her strongest admirers recognize that Engel signally failed to exploit the character of Mrs. Saxe, who, although intended to serve as catalyst and *deus ex machina*, remains a one-dimensional cutout doll, patently a device that falls far short of acquiring any convincingly felt life.[50]

Engel's relative success in handling everything else is disputed. Some commentators praise her "sense of place";[51] another complains that ". . . after the really intriguing opening, . . . the sense of place curiously dissipates."[52] Some revel in her enormous and vital cast of secondary characters, while others lament their "flatness," "boring inevitability," and failure to be "very interesting."[53] Her handling of narrative technique receives conflicting assessment, particularly the manner in which she does — or doesn't! — make excessive use of lengthy interior monologues and dialogue to fill in narrative gaps.[54] And the fact that the novel's actions are neither released nor ordered into a tight and coherent framework irritates some with its disarray,[55] yet strikes others as an apt structural complement to its central themes.[56]

Because *The Tattooed Woman* was published just four months after the writer's death in February of 1985, this group of reviews is singular: many reviewers pay tribute to her life and work; some prematurely attempt to place the Engel canon within Canadian literary history. Book reviewers often exhibit uncharacteristic good manners — perhaps issuing from twinges of guilt over their past neglect and unkind reviews — in the face of such an untimely death; their more hyperbolic statements of praise are likely to give way in time to more temperate assessments. And although this second short-story collection has received higher acclaim than *Inside the Easter Egg*, nonetheless it elicited that striking degree of ambivalence generally characteristic of critical responses to Engel's fiction.

On the fulsome side fall such remarks as these: ". . . *The Tattooed Woman* proves that Marian Engel's short fiction was as skilful and moving as any in Canadian literature"; [57] "Marian Engel's superb collection of 16 stories ranks beside or above the best of her novels . . . and assures her a place among Canada's leading writers of fiction." [58] About this same "brilliant book, absolutely dazzling," [59] others are less enthusiastic: "Unfortunately . . . *The Tattooed Woman* is a somewhat flat close to a notable opus"; [60] and "the collection is too uneven for unreserved praise." [61] Critical evaluation of the merits of individual stories also fluctuates wildly. While a few stories are singled out with some consistency as exceptionally good, each also has its detractors.

That critics and reviewers may hold conflicting estimations of the overall stature of a novelist is not uncommon, but, over a seventeen-year span to so markedly disagree about her characteristic strengths and weaknesses, to so strikingly dispute which books are even noteworthy, *is* unusual. It is not surprising that Marian Engel made what only appears to be an arbitrary distinction between her critics and her readers: "Well, at one point you have to make a conscious decision — and that is, who your audience is . . . . I had to decide — quickly — not to write for academics . . . . I suppose that I wrote for my peers . . . other women of my generation" (Matyas and Joiner, p. 5). To the end of her life, she was content to see her work simply judged by a jury of those "peers."

Engel's Works

Marian Engel, speaking in 1981, admitted that *No Clouds of Glory* gave her "a slight sense of embarrassment . . . . I have become, as I've got older, more conservative and more technically proficient" (Corbeil, p. 3). Yet her first novel deserves attention for its serious (if disjunctive) pursuit of humane social values and its satiric indictment of contemporary bourgeois mores, particularly as they affect women. *No Clouds of Glory* also offers some penetrating insights into the determination of personality by early environment; this subject, along with Engel's use of place as a correlative for mental states, portends the mature novelist. Although her voice is not uniformly assured here, the writing reveals frequent glimpses of the stylistic strengths that enliven her later fiction.

The novel's essential immaturity is structurally manifest in its fractured form. It ultimately reduces to a series of disconnected existential speculations. To explore the subject of identity, Engel uses a recurrent metaphor of opposition: the conflict between romanticism and reality. The metaphor fails to function as an organizing principle because the narrative too vigorously insists upon a radical demarcation between these two elements. Thus it fails to provide a deeply felt investigation into their shattering conjunction in Sarah Porlock's life. By sustaining the central dialogue on this strictly dialectical basis, *No Clouds of Glory* uncertainly gestures in two directions at once — towards a romantic ideal of passionate personal existence and a half-hearted engagement with "scrofulous" reality. This nervous vacillation has its origins in Engel's characterization of her narrator-protagonist and in Sarah's restrictive viewpoint. Both, in turn, contribute to the reduction to almost caricature value of the symbolic settings and minor characters.

The novel is confessional in form and content. "I should begin at the beginning if there were one, but all beginnings belong inside people, and my reading of my own entrails has been unscientific," says the narrator at the outset; but adds immediately: "I keep having to remind myself that I shall not improve. Unchristian, but true. You always stay what you are. Fortunately, you do not have to stay where you are."[62] Her autobiographical undertaking takes the form spelled out in Engel's original choice of title, *Sarah Bastard's Notebook.*[63] She structures her literary record to fit the way she recollects her experience. By "unscientifically" fracturing her sense of time and place, her notebook mirrors the confusions and illogicalities inherent in her perceptions of her past. Engel further manipulates viewpoint to reveal the progressive emergence of Sarah's behavioural "patterns": ". . . what I trail behind me is not clouds of glory [i.e., a "bucolic childhood"] . . . but memories of my own patterns" (p. 114). *Patterns* provide the clue to her identity as a "psychological determinist": "The things I do as pitifully inevitable beside the product that I am" (p. 122).

To articulate this concept of personality, Engel juxtaposes analogous or parallel events as they collide in Sarah's consciousness: her sister's elopement with Sandro and her own affair with him, her relationship with her mother and with the maternal Dr. Lyle, for example. Autobiographical history repeats itself with only minor variations. Hence her protracted "reading of [her] own entrails" has only a limited, *predictive* utility. She finds herself "looking as usual in the past for Sarah's future" (p. 49). For this reason, plot is not a

strong unifying element in the narrative. Sarah's intense
and her divided consciousness dictate the plotting of the actic.
dislocated, attenuated fashion. This has the advantage of allowing
her to record truthfully the doubts and contradictions of her experience. Perhaps because she is a literary person, she is often tempted to
cast her romantic aspirations (pathetically denied in her love affairs)
into the elevating forms of fable, fairy tale, myth, legend, and
parable.[64] However, she rejects these dishonest representations as
the "corruption of reality into romanticism" (p. 70). What she is left
with is a selfhood in a constant state of metamorphosis: "I go on
watching, and in myself melting and re-forming day after day"
(p. 12).

Ultimately Sarah's mind becomes the novel's most sharply realized
setting; the skeletal plot is charted along the intricately shifting
topography of her interior landscape. This mental site is so keenly
self-actualizing that it colours her myopic memories of people and
place to the degree that they become mere functions of her will —
either as projections of her romantic ideals or as validations of her
misanthropic sense of reality. Through the ideal (romantic) and
debased (satiric) extremes of fictional portrayal, she subverts her
original autobiographical intention and becomes the novelist of her
own life. She openly declares her unreliability as a narrator: "a gos-
sip of secondhand values and an impressive range of half-truths"
(p. 115). "Scraping down to the facts," for which she has no aptitude,
"is a lifework in an age of turgid prose" (p. 155).

In Sarah Porlock we see the outlines of Marian Engel's typical heroine. She is a spirited, well-educated woman on a collision course
with the male-dominant world. Fatal to her sense of identity is her
ambivalence about being a woman: "And of course I cannot, though
I have tried to, in my own consciousness, change the fact that I am a
woman" (p. 115). Her personal acts of rebellion against the sexism
and materialism of her society are perversely predicated upon the
very values she, in reality, has internalized. When her political-libi-
dinal (the terms are synonymous in Engel's world) imagination
tempts her to break through those repressive constraints, the conse-
quences are always the same: guilt for the deed done or a submissive
deference to male preference. She regards biology as the psycho-
sexual determinant of female compliance: "The good thing about
men is being under them, subordinated; it gives you a sense of where
you belong — biologically and for always" (p. 48). By failing to

distinguish between sex (what is given) and gender (a relative, cultu-
rally imposed concept), she accedes to conventional female stereoty-
ping. Just as her rigid polarization of human sexuality into
"masculine" and "feminine" components deprives her of satisfactory heterosexual relationships,[65] so her polarization of female sexuality into "bull dike" (p. 22) and womanly elements blinds her to the
unconventional side of her own nature. Her fear of becoming, or
being perceived as, a lesbian is so intense that it runs like an unconscious leitmotif throughout her recollections.[66] As a direct conse-
quence of her dialectical habits of mind, she is incapable of devising
for herself a comfortable identity. She cannot "learn to resolve"
(p. 141) and so remains trapped between her compensatory romanti-
cisms — "making myths, legends, or monuments" — and her reduc-
tive realisms — "a screw is a screw is a screw" (p. 155).

The dualities of self are objectified in the stereotyped dualities of
place. Although firmly committed to the notion that "where you
are" is subject to the exercise of her will, "where Sarah is" at various
points in her life seems almost irrelevant. Setting is merely a locus for
her state of mind. Whatever existential potential might inhere in any
given landscape is overwhelmed by her tendency to project onto it
her shifting states of schizoid alienation (from reality) or sympathetic
identification (with romance). The "real" world is located in Canada, specifically in the "small, scorned [southwestern Ontario]
places" (p. 131) of her upbringing and in Toronto, which also
"rejects the subconscious" (p. 10). Engel's interest in depicting these
locales is grounded in how their Puritanism affected the young
Sarah; she is not concerned with the precise observation of regional
speech and behaviour or with the concrete particularities of her
settings. What we are given is a sense of place as shorthand notation,
an imaginative approximation of the arid and ungiving contours of
Queen Victoria's mind.

The novelist's descriptive strategies radically change in her
portrayal of the "lyric north" (p. 17) where Sarah spent her summers
at her grandfather's cottage. This world is ironically depicted in
classically lush romantic images: "A ship, an isle, a sickle moon: all
the claptrap" (p. 18). The novel derives its overall stylistic texture
from this constant, jarring juxtaposition of tonal surfaces. Two
clearly discernible styles emerge which respectively mirror the novel's
two major points of reference: an unblinkered naturalism, which
captures the sordid empirical details of the real world, and a classical

lyricism, which keeps the romantic bubbles afloat. The following description, with its tensely opposed terms, prefigures the manner in which Engel later uses the European and Toronto settings to symbolize the two orders of experience:

> . . . those of us who grow up in romantic scenery continue subject to its dangerous charm. We carpeted our afternoon with Swedes, Norwegians, Australians, Americans, Canadians, Russians: inheritors of grandeur and space, forever because of it sentimental. The poetry of the land drives us away from living; we try instead to construct epics; early, our diseased consciousness seeks the remote and exotic, there are always the mountains on the horizon, blinding us to extant reality, which we think of as worms. We cannot describe our surroundings without encrusting them with sugar; we speak another generation's hyperbole and deny there is evil in the happy land. (p. 19)
> — what ?

Even as she reconstructs the idyll, Sarah warns herself not "to get caught again in that romance, to tell again the story of everyone's blissful Canuck childhood: little well-fed kings and queens against a landscape" (p. 21). Yet she allows her fantasy to become incarnate in the person of Sandro, her brother-in-law, with whom she has a Harlequin-romance-style affair on a Mediterranean island, the "location of paradise." She exalts it into a "land of myth" in which everything — "the sea and the sun and the sand and the surf, earth, sea, and sky; moon, june; sex" (p. 108) — conspires to lure her into a self-destructive myth about their relationship. The lyrical evocation of the island and the entire allusive network of romantic imagery disintegrate utterly with the "seepage of reality" (p. 89) into the fantasy.

At the conclusion of the novel, Sarah devises a geographical solution to her dilemma. She rejects Toronto, "the city that festers with subcutaneous infection . . . . founded by interest and fostered by denial" (p. 117), for Montreal, where "pride, intelligence and corruption have mated and produced not despair but revolution" (p. 152). In effect she chooses to become an expatriate in her native country. Quebec's sense of emergent destiny clearly has a romantic appeal for someone who cannot define her own nature. For Sarah, Montreal becomes a Canadian version of Europe — as yet unknown and unexperienced, and therefore susceptible to being mythologized. Like any good determinist, she has come viciously full circle in her substitution of one myth of place for another. Her muted statement of belief at the novel's close strikes an unwittingly ominous note: "Jump, or you'll die, Sarah. And there'll never be green landscape or a sweet face again" (p. 181).

The final note of indeterminacy suggests that Engel did not quite know how to dispose of Sarah; it is as if the novelist were uneasy about the book's failure either to commit itself to, or disengage itself from, the heroine's romantic idealism. Minn Burge, heroine of *The Honeyman Festival*, repeats the same pattern, although she is more aware than Sarah of the basic hostility of experience to that kind of idealism. Paradoxically, she is more desperately in need of it. She attempts to counterbalance her romanticism by grounding herself in the dismal realities of family life — the very source of her need to fantasize.

The thematic and technical parallels between the two novels are striking. The second novel features a first-person narrator-protagonist who is questing backwards over the key events in her personal life in order to comprehend her present alienation. The contours of her past are remarkably like Sarah's: again there are three distinct settings with similar meanings as conditioning elements — southwestern Ontario, Toronto, and Europe. Minn's banal existence as a wife and mother stands in sharp relief to the lost romantic dream of lover-in-Europe. Like Sarah, she swings erratically between the dialectical extremes of reality and an illusory ideal, "floundering in flux,"[67] with no perception of any composing harmony. Again the heroine's identity conflict is held in contrapuntal tension through the opposition of romantic/realistic imagery, but with a significant difference. In *The Honeyman Festival*, film replaces symbolisms of place as the central metaphorical nucleus around which the governing polarities are grouped. The settings are realized sparsely — almost notationally — with few symbolic elaborations. Engel has made a strong shift from outer to inward reference in her second book, but its basic design, and the vision of experience it implies, remain constant. Minn's interior monologues, like Sarah's, serve two functions: as formal representations of her mental solitude; and as the means whereby diverse moments of experience are juxtaposed, as associative memory composes them, to reveal recurrent patterns.

The Honeyman Festival has an even more concentrated unity of action; the time scheme is reduced to approximately twelve hours. The novel opens at 7:00 P.M. as Minn takes a hot bath prior to preparing for her party to mark the closing night of the seventh annual Honeyman Film Festival; it closes in the early hours of the following morning as Minn reads *The Globe and Mail* over coffee. Each of the thirteen chapters has a central action, an intrinsically insignificant activity drawn from Minn's domestic routine. These mundane activities serve as Proustian triggers to memory: Minn hears "time ticking around her, beginning to expand" (p. 2). But whereas the complex workings of involuntary memory served Proust as a key to the truth of experience, shaping it into art, the reality that gradually defines itself here remains without any coherent schematization. In the novel's final words, reality itself is thrown into question as the protagonist challenges even the empirical grounds of her investigation: "And the morning will come, and so will the night again. Won't it?" (p. 131).

The central metaphor through which Minn "images" her investigation is film. Engel's extended use of the metaphor considerably widens the thematic context by offering a visual correlative as richly textured as her similarly functioning descriptions of setting in *No Clouds of Glory*. The recurrent cinematic allusions provide Minn with a framing device — in effect a camera — through which she can "shoot" her perceptions. Like her absentee husband, she uses "the movies" as escapism "when she [does] not want reality to interfere with her attempts to maintain a poetic view of life" (p. 126). But because she is in an "imprisoned situation" (p. 5), her movies are all *interior*: "The mind has molehills and they lead to tunnels of escape" (p. 96). Her "personal never-never land" has a counterpart in the "silly stories about never-never land" (p. 41) once filmed by her ex-lover, the director Honeyman. She "shoots" her past as film in the "landscape of her imagination" (p. 104), describing its manifestations in cinematic images.

This aspect of the novel has been explored by Douglas H. Parker in "'Memories of My Own Patterns': Levels of Reality in *The Honeyman Festival*." The essay is useful for its exhaustive catalogue of film images; however, Parker's interpretation of the cluster of meanings generated by the metaphor is simplistic and misleading. He comments that, "for Minn, the difference between her ['unhappy'] childhood and her days with Honeyman ['her happy past in Paris'] is the difference between the all too real and the romantic genres of the film" (p. 113). Minn's "new awareness" when she "identifies for the first time the nature of reality" follows "her exorcism of the world of film"; this he interprets as her turning from "her unsuccessful attempts at escape, which simulate the kind of world that Honeyman created for her, to the services of humanity and the care of the oppressed" (p. 115).

Now, one of Marian Engel's great strengths as a writer — a strength that has cost her dearly in terms of reputation — is her insistence upon reporting truthfully the contradictions implicit in a mutable and relativistic world. Apart from *Bear*, her novels are not small masterpieces of dramatic economy; they stoutly resist such diagrammatic forms as Parker imposes on *The Honeyman Festival*. Minn comments in this spirit: ". . . it disgusted her when people wanted to divide the world into two sides and ignore its multifariousness" (p. 75). The novel reveals the gradual breakdown of Minn's polarizations as she subjects them to a more dispassionate scrutiny. In fact, Engel handles her dualities and their symbolic referents with far more sophistication than she did in her first novel. Minn does not "exorcise the world of the film"; she puts her lingering romantic obsessions with Honeyman into a new perspective by relating what she has always known about the kind of filmmaker he was to the "kind of world that Honeyman created for her." And it is not a question of distinguishing between "real" and "romantic" genres of film. Honeyman's films — "horse operas," "Italian comic books," "French piracies of history" (p. 17) — were formulaic entertainments that reflected the surfaces of life: "He crafted it, but he didn't open it up at the end, he wasn't an artist, he was only interested in the finite" (p. 97). They were, in short, "movies" as opposed to "film art."

However therapeutic her relationship with this "father-figure" may have been in liberating Minn from the "heathen blanket of southern Ontario guilt" (p. 14), her so-called "happy past" with him is *identical* to her "unhappy" present. She experiences both her relationship with Honeyman and with her husband as a prison which shuts her off from vital contact with the world, a degrading submission to male domination. Honeyman kept her literally imprisoned during their five-year affair. She describes her marriage as "captivity," and childbearing in metaphors of sexual slavery: "Concubine on delivery table, strapped, helpless: a little touch of Honeyman in the night. And in the day, crap-scrubbing" (p. 46). Like Sarah

Porlock, Minn repeats in her maturity the pattern of subservience that characterized her youthful affairs with men.

Finally, Parker's statement that Minn rejects the "world of the film" ignores the richly allusive uses to which Engel puts her metaphor. Minn's expatriate years in Paris coincide with the inception of the *nouvelle vague* movement, that sudden influx of new talent into French cinema that issued in François Truffaut's *The 400 Blows*, *Shoot the Piano Player*, and *Jules and Jim*; Jean-Luc Godard's *Breathless*; and Alain Resnais's *Hiroshima Mon Amour* and *Last Year at Marienbad*.[68] Minn refers directly to the key principle behind the movement, the *auteur* theory: ". . . before she went to France she hadn't known that films had directors the way books have authors" (p. 6); and after her party she acknowledges that "Honeyman is dead. Godard is the great film maker" (p. 97). Her aesthetic sympathies are clearly on the side of the serious filmmakers who, unlike Honeyman, eschew the commercial packages of the huge studios. In one important scene, she recalls her hometown: ". . . the sound-and-light show of her subconscious sent flickering across her vacant mind the images of Godwin as if it were the only frame of reference she had ever known . . . . [I]t rose before her again, more real and larger than ever before, like a movie . . . . [S]he began to see it in frames" (p. 40). As she reconstructs this childhood memory, she shoots it *cinéma vérité* fashion by filming her subjects as unobtrusively and uninterruptedly as possible. But she quickly discovers that the documentary approach does not move towards the disclosure of anything "meaningful." "Life did not make art," she complains (p. 44). Only by distorting reality through the imposition of Honeyman-type effects can the filmmaker establish a sense of design: "But you'd want something bigger and more dramatic to make a film, the big lurching movement to climax or fall. Something that had a recognizable pattern, something clear" (p. 43). By having Minn reject such fraudulent aesthetic devices, Engel implies that the devices of mimetic realism are the only legitimate means of exploring reality, which cannot be shot "with vaseline on the lens" (p. 47).

The world of *The Honeyman Festival* is limited to that of the observing and recording self. It is important to determine how fully this total inwardness succeeds in conveying the complex nature of the reality Engel scrutinizes. Three reviewers complained of these severe restrictions; their criticism is based on an assumption that the novelist should have devised for her protagonist a design for living that corresponds to the conceptual form of the novel — that some coherent world view should emerge from the aesthetic blueprint.[69] Minn unhappily recognizes that, once stripped of romanticism, neither art nor life yields a "design." However, much as one appreciates Engel's fidelity to her own vision of experience, one *is* left with the feeling that her inquiry is somehow not conducted with the degree of intellectual rigour it demands. The novel sets the theme of identity in too narcissistic a frame of reference. Minn's sole act of rebellion, a hysterical attack on a policeman, is an atypical response to bourgeois mores; it springs from her immature need to rebel rather than from a thoughtful rejection of established social values: it is "an attempt to infuse drama, vision of a final victory over respectability" (p. 115). Her inability to relate her oppression to that of other people, especially to women who share her plight, leads her to collaborate in her own victimization. On these grounds, one doubts not only her ability to even minimally transform her marriage; her attainment of a successful female selfhood is also unlikely.

Engel might have enlarged her perspective by coupling Minn's concern with identity and reality with a more probing examination of the nature and function of film. Were Minn a filmmaker herself, for example, rather than a dilettante whose essentially thin speculations about the form cause her to reiterate variations of the same question without any deepening clarification, filmmaking could serve as rich a thematic and metaphoric function as writing does in, say, Margaret Laurence's *The Diviners*, Alice Munro's *Lives of Girls and Women*, Margaret Atwood's *Lady Oracle*, or Audrey Thomas' *Latakia*. Minn, however, has no sense of vocation to mediate between her perception of the inadequacy of reality and her correspondingly nihilistic viewpoint: "Each day I wake *tabula rasa* except for the blurred smudging of dreams" (p. 53). Unlike Morag Gunn or Del Jordan, she has no artistic function to place in organic relationship with the rest of life and is unable to assume the prerogative of imposing a viewpoint on her impressions: "There's no action for me, no direction. Everything is confused and flaccid" (p. 47). To the end of the novel, she remains a camera in search of a director.

"Here, with air above and sea below, . . . he should have written poems here. Though he wasn't fond of place as subject-matter, he said it was a cop-out. He wanted to get above himself, out of his skin into ideas."[70] So remarks the protagonist of *Monodromos* about her poet-lover's feelings concerning "place as subject-matter."

Ironically, it is precisely this thematic conception that best describes Engel's intention in her third novel. Her underlying motivation seems to have been to "get above" her heroine's self-absorption, "into ideas" about the collision of progress and tradition in modern Cyprus, the strains inherent in a binational country, the role of women in a patriarchal culture, and the intersection of the realm of art with the sensual world. While she was writing *Monodromos*, Engel remarked in an interview that she was concerned with the problem, as the interviewer phrased it, of being "thrown back increasingly upon a personal view of the world": ". . . after doing *No Clouds of Glory* and *The Honeyman Festival*, I got very uptight about using too much of myself" (Gibson, p. 96). She attempted to overcome this subjectivity — and, by implication, the strong autobiographical component — of her two earlier novels by shifting the locus of narrative attention from character to setting, from an interest in interior landscapes and personal identity to a complex meditation upon place and cultural identity.

The novel represents Engel's first attempt to dispassionately examine the Mediterranean setting, free from the romantic stereotypes which previously surrounded it. Audrey Moore's quest is for an *escape* from personality, to "know both the city and the island like an encyclopaedia" (p. 38). Gone is the heroine's preoccupation with distinguishing reality from romance — and with it the obsession with her past and her fantasy world. Audrey's focus is on what lies directly in front of her in the vital present; she wants to capture the "multiplicity" of the place without forcing upon it a consistency of meaning or dialectical framework. Upon discovering the true historical identity of Cleopatra, she observes: "The world falls apart, reassembles itself, falls apart again, and you discover that Cleopatra was a Macedonian Greek and the kaleidoscope turns" (p. 133). The kaleidoscope is an apt image for describing Engel's method of portraying Cyprus. The narrative swarms with details drawn from landscape and topography; architecture; local culinary delights; history, literature, and travel guides; social customs; and patterns of speech. With this steady massing and proliferation of detail, fact slips into legend, apocrypha become truth; history is subjected to endless revisions. In Audrey's kaleidoscopic documentation of the reality of place, the "pieces" of Cyprus are always becoming equivocal, dissolving, fusing — unlike that typically Byzantine mode of art, the mosaic, in which each separate piece retains its identity.

Audrey comes to realize that her quest for the meaning of the island has not been successful: "I'm one of those opaque lady travellers after all, who sees, but does not understand" (p. 237). The novelist suggests that her protagonist's failure to "understand" is linked to Audrey's inability to create a recognizable individuality, that the processes of coming to know *who* one is and *where* one is are inextricably bound. Audrey's failures are failures of vision: merely to observe is not to see into the nature of reality. This is not the first time Engel has written about the limitations of perception and of empirically based views of the "real" world; both Sarah and Minn were acutely conscious of the emptiness of "extant reality" shorn of imaginative transformation. But one sensed in those books that the novelist faulted reality itself. *Monodromos* presents a considerable advance on this view — one that enables the novelist to deal more satisfactorily with the nature of personality in her subsequent characterizations. Here she locates part of the problem in *how* Audrey sees, in effect, through a faulty lens: "The place keeps going in and out of focus on me" (p. 107); and "'Everything's turned from coloured to grey for me. I'm haunted by the idea . . . . That I've done — no, seen — the wrong things, or been the wrong person. That I haven't noticed enough. Or noticed the right things'" (p. 201). Her frustrated compulsion "to hold the world together with [her] eyes" (p. 201), expressed earlier as a need to "build a composite view of this place" (p. 107), is an expression of the modern artistic dilemma. If no absolute frame of reference exists, then the conventional notion of perspective (which structured its images of reality to address a single spectator) no longer obtains. Audrey, however, still attempts to play God with Cyprus; the "composite view" to which she aspires is negated because her single perspective — the "camera" in her head — is relative to her position in time and space. The visible world, in constant flux, remains fugitive. She further compounds the problem by narrowing her viewpoint to what she *allows* herself to see: "I have travelled and seen nothing, listened, and heard nothing. The lenses and membranes are fitted wrong, they're the wrong brand, no. . . . it's not that one doesn't understand. It is that one does not want to understand" (p. 238).

Many modern and post-modern novelists have attempted to capture the relativity of perception by experimenting with multiple viewpoints; they show character and event in relation to several angles of vision.[71] Engel's decision to retain the first person as narrative centre is related to her thematic concern with the obliquity of vision. Her narrator forcibly limits the boundaries of perspective by refusing to search for what lies beyond. She remains locked within the walls of private experience out of fearfulness and because she is walled within the confines of gender in a society that has never tolerated female independence. Thus her failure to "know" Cyprus is double-edged: she is self-oppressed and oppressed by the male/female polarization of society. The resulting conscription of her life there is echoed in the street sign on her block: "TEK YOL/MONO-DROMOS/ONE WAY STREET" (p. 7).

Rather than duplicating the rigid symbolic algebras of *No Clouds of Glory* and *The Honeyman Festival* that corresponded to her thematic dualities, Engel uses metaphor in a minor key in *Monodromos* to express an ambivalent, rather than binary, viewpoint. The metaphor of walls serves as a concrete correlative for her imprisonment. The description of the city's walls that opens the novel (p. 1) is repeated with variation at the end (pp. 240–41). Shortly after her arrival, Audrey fails in her attempt "to circumnavigate the walls" (p. 2) — just as she ultimately will fail to circumnavigate them imaginatively. The walls make "a strong image for the place, tie it together" (p. 3); they also make a "strong image" for her predicament: "In this society I am handicapped by my femininity, I can't take on any male enterprise at all; but I am fairly contented to be surrounded by walls . . . . [W]alls are a comforting form of psychic limit. I feel less exposed than I would in an unwalled town on the plain" (pp. 79–80). She is imprisoned within an island culture and, in violating its sexual code by taking a lover, finds herself forcibly "islanded" within her own house. In the pivotal chapter, entitled "Heat," the oppressive midsummer climate and an oppressive situation come together; an ancient Greek woman, "a lone Eumenide" (p. 138), stations herself outside of the khan, refusing to let Audrey leave. She is under the mistaken impression that her captive's lover is her married grandson. Nonetheless, Audrey's Puritan conscience responds to this "centuries old" embodiment of guilt in terms that recall Minn Burge's image of uterine captivity: "She makes me sweat with nervousness and shame. She takes my worries and embodies them. She takes me off the hot sun-stinging streets and puts me back into the condition I was conceived in: a warm enclosure . . . . The walls are thick, the doors are thick. I am a prisoner, but I am also safe" (pp. 139–40). She concludes that leaving the womb is pointless:

"All my life I've been trying to discover some reason for the surge of activity my birth plunged me into" (p. 141). She does concede, however, that the islanders' lives are anchored in meanings she cannot comprehend: "There has to be more to that big abstraction we call life for want of a better word . . ., there is more, the people here know it. But I don't know what it is" (p. 237).

Throughout the novel, her quest for the meaning of the island is linked to her search for the "ikon of the dog-headed saint," a pagan relic of an animal-God. "[T]o know the authorship of the dog-headed saint would be to know the island" (p. 152), suggests her lover, Max. This key image is sustained by a subtly related minor metaphor; on three occasions, Audrey describes Cyprus as an "old yellow dog of an island snoozing in the sun, tail rucking the armpit of Asia Minor" (p. 174; cf. pp. 245, 246–47). Her play upon the dog analogy links the mythic past of the island, conjured by the richly connotative word *Byzantium*, with its present modern phase when, at the conclusion of *Monodromos*, the symbolic meanings converge in the image of a young dancing boy. The novelist does not want the ikon to "mean" in a strictly aesthetic sense as, for example, does Yeats' golden bird in "Sailing to Byzantium" — a poem to which Audrey makes explicit reference: "Poets don't known the domesticity of Byzantium, they're all too busy looking for mosaics, gyres and mechanical birds" (p. 37). She acknowledges that, while its "charm" belongs to the "conjunction of images," "all the poetry that ever tried to exist" (p. 38), the meaning of the place cannot reside, as it did for Yeats, in "monuments of unageing intellect."[72] The island is "not a monument but a whole place with its evolution showing" (p. 38). Yeats' Byzantium is the city of perfected art, a symbol of the spiritual life absolutely divorced from sensuality; as the permanence of the artist is enshrined in the perfection of his artifices, so (by immodest implication) is the immortality of the poet in the perfection of his word-smithery. Engel's narrator, on the other hand, makes the post-modern observation that "I notice that when you take this place apart with words it ceases to exist" (p. 38). Far from transmuting reality into a Platonic Form, language destroys it.

But the novelist has only the resources of language to convey meaning. Engel comes very close to articulating the ineffable identity of Cyprus through the beautiful image of the dancing boy and a related musical analogy, which trace a continuity between historic, mythic Cyprus and its "modern version." The face of this androgynous figure of superlative loveliness recalls the ikon of the dogheaded saint: "The smile is the smile on the face of an idol. . . . the smile of a snake." Like the ikon, he summons into memory "heresies and visions and infinite, mocking subtlety." His meanings are cryptic, as elusive and tantalizing as Cyprus itself. His dance represents an instinctual rebuttal of Yeatsian Unity of Being: "This boy has been taught to remember the old — not wholeness, but chaos." The "eery notes" of the "strange music" to which he dances echo the complex nature of Becoming: "The music is more piercing than the music they usually make here, it exists even in the intervals of their minor scale." Cyprus is a chaotic rendition of "all mixtures," caught between pagan and modern, Greek and Turk (symbolized architecturally in the monasteries and mosques), history and progress (symbolized in the dilapidated khan and the "Bauhaus skyscraper"), the Homeric tradition and the Christian. And like the dancing boy, Cyprus embodies the antinomies without succumbing to the Western compulsion "to ease the strain of multiplicity" (pp. 238–39).

Audrey tells herself before leaving the island that "landscape is meaningless, . . . it doesn't matter where you live, it matters how" (p. 245). And although she is warned by a Cypriot, "Do not mourn for that island, it is not a person, only a place" (p. 250), one suspects that she will continue to mourn the place after she has returned to England, where, she says, "For a long time I haunt olive merchants, speaking to them in borrowed words" (p. 250).

Owing to its peculiar genesis, Engel's fourth novel, *Joanne*, represents something of an anomaly within the oeuvre. It was originally commissioned as a radio script, "a serial novel to be written on the spot,"[73] and received only minor revisions prior to its publication. CBC's *This Country in the Morning* broadcast it in four-minute daily episodes, five days a week for thirteen weeks. *Joanne* does not merit — nor can it stand up to — the kind of intensive analysis one applies to Engel's more "serious" work. Its primary interest resides in the thematic expansion given the subject of male/female relationships — a subject that becomes the major focus of her next two novels — and in its trek over familiar Engel terrain, small-town southwestern Ontario. Finally, it seems likely that the exigencies of writing to such an abbreviated format served her as apprenticeship for the stylistic and dramatic economy of *Bear*.

The basic pattern of the novel corresponds roughly to the broadcast schedule, with Joanne recording entries in her diary five days a week over a fourteen-week period. The first half of her diary chronicles the "final days" of her eighteen-year-old marriage to Bill Laurence, which is brought to an abrupt climax when his mother kidnaps their two children; the second half charts her move from Toronto to a small town where she regains her independence and begins "a new life." Although Engel notes in her Preface that the popular Victorian tradition of serial writing produced such superb fictions as Wilkie Collins' *The Moonstone*, *Joanne* is singularly lacking in the quality that the mode best realized: the creation of a suspenseful atmosphere generated by a fast-paced plot and dramatically punctuated by a series of climaxes. The severe linearity of the pattern, and the division of the action into the discrete units of daily entry, work against the kind of structure that Engel more comfortably devises for her novels. Gone are the larger architectural rhythms, the tight dialectical design, and the symbolic or metaphoric elaborations of theme. The result is a "thin," episodic rendering of experience. The novelist attempted to overcome this problem by building "with vignettes and epiphanies" (Pref., n. pag.), techniques of compression which she uses in the manner of Dickensian "signatures" to establish her minor characters, like Rosie the chicken eviscerator (pp. 92–93) or Joanne's cousin Faber (p. 116).

While the diary form allows for the presentation of the immediate impact of events upon the protagonist, the hastily improvised nature of these events mitigates against any satisfactory deliberation upon them. Unlike Engel's earlier heroines, though, Joanne's character is dramatically modified in the course of the narrative: she changes from a casebook example of the oppressed bourgeois housewife into a casebook, strong, self-determining, "liberated heroine." The novel makes frequent explicit references to "women's lib" (see pp. 7, 15, 20, 44, 101); and Joanne is forced to work her way through all the detritus of marital breakdown (litigation over alimony, child custody, and the division of property; reentry into the work force, etc.). She begs for female reader identification. Her actions are exemplary in their adherence to the uplifting advice offered in feminist self-help books — she takes positive, self-assertive actions — but her story is only a confirming footnote adduced to the experience of going it alone.

Joanne resembles Sarah Porlock and Minn Burge in that she pays lip service to the focal topics of feminist analysis while inadvertently revealing herself as having internalized patriarchal values. The most telling example of her retrograde thinking is her inability as a mother to distinguish between learned and innate behaviours in her son and daughter (see pp. 106–07). In one important respect, her characterization marks an advance on those of Sarah and Minn; because she has some sense of the politics of personal experience, the novel contains a stronger element of social criticism. But the potential force of her awareness is inhibited by her habitually muddled apprehensions. In her flashbacks to her mother's poverty-wracked life, and in her memories of her Trotskyite Aunt Frieda, she shows a sensitivity to the roots of oppression in the class system; she continually contrasts her own "low life" origins on a depression farm to her husband's Rosedale background; she is acutely aware of the sexist power plays that turned her marriage into a "rape game" (p. 45); and she observes how capitalism invites its victims to collaborate in their own degradation: "I have this theory that behind consumerdom lies the motive of keeping the people busy buying things so they won't think about politics" (p. 86). Yet for all this, she is unable to perceive any connections among capitalism, colonialism, and the oppression of women: "But sometimes I wonder if, considering the status of Africans, the status of women isn't a fairly decadent issue" (p. 92). The novel offers ample confirmation of Joanne's assessment of herself as a "shallow" and "pretty vapid woman" (p. 44).

The overall lack of distinction of the nineteen stories collected in *Inside the Easter Egg* largely stems from the fact that the novelist's characteristic way of conceiving a fiction works against the tight construction and concentrated brevity that most commonly define the short story. Engel once confessed, "I don't know why the genre doesn't fit me in any special way" (Gibson, p. 90). The reason is clear: Engel is a writer who needs space. She is at her best working with "the bigness and the challenge and the complexity, and the looseness" of fiction in its expansive form (Gibson, p. 90). Her characters need room to stretch; in the stories they have sufficient compass only to flex a muscle. Other short-story writers (for example, Alice Munro and Mavis Gallant) rise to the challenge by revealing character through small-scale, yet deeply allusive, incidents. Engel seems to lack their facility for telegraphic delineation. Stripped of the exegetical complexity bestowed on their counterparts in her novels, her characters stand as sketches for a stillborn novel.

The problem is as much thematic as technical, having to do with the tunnel vision the writer brings to bear on her story material. The interwoven thematic contraries of the first three novels give way in the stories to single strands of meaning, and dialectical tension is abandoned for a homogeneous, one-dimensional world view, distressingly bourgeois in character. One has no sense of characters being provoked out of their complacencies, of received ideas being seriously challenged. This flaw has its most telling revelation in five of the stories that comprise the first group, titled "The Married Life" (I omit "Amaryllis," the mood and background context of which more appropriately fit into the second group, "Ziggy and Company"). They should be taken into consideration along with three stories from the third section, "Children and Ancestors" — "Meredith and the Lousy Latin Lover," "Only God, My Dear," and "The Fall of the House That Jack Built." (The imperfect tripartite grouping of this collection suggests that either the editor or writer was hoping that the cumulative effect of each section would buttress the individual, weak stories within it; this attempt to give an impression of unity and resonance to what are, in reality, very disparate, meandering stories fails simply because they are unsupported by the kind of organic coherence that links, for example, the stories comprising Alice Munro's *Lives of Girls and Women*.)

Although these eight stories are narrated as third-person interior monologue, a distinct persona nonetheless emerges: a woman in the middle phase of her bourgeois marital partnership, unhappy with the burdens imposed on her by domesticity and motherhood. Her intensely inner view is more congenial to a novel like *The Honeyman Festival*; here it gets in the way of more effective revelation through scene and dialogue. "The Salt Mines" best epitomizes the weaknesses of this loose grouping of "Married Life" stories. Ostensibly it is about the "quality of guilt"[74] surrounding the adulterous behaviour of its narrator, Ruth, married for twenty boring years to a lawyer. It inadvertently becomes a parable of co-option, of the rejection of freedom (symbolized in the instinctual life) for the compensating amenities of status and security that make marriage endurable. Ruth's extramarital affair is a brief rebellion against the vacancy and tedium of married life, her momentary incursion into a lost dream of romance. The life-denying but self-serving economic character of her marriage blunts the reader's compassionate respect for her dilemma. The story has no cutting edge: we're dealing here with a world of surfaces, middle-class family life only briefly disturbed by a midlife resurgence of lust. The narrator is class-conscious to the extent that she knows where *she* belongs. A mood of cheerless lassitude dominates all of these stories, as do the undifferentiated, droning voices of the self-absorbed narrators. They are anecdotes without depth, told without the vital cadence and movement that action and dialogue might have imparted.

The stories of the middle section, "Ziggy and Company," centre on the character of Ziggy, a peripatetic social anthropologist. Engel's portrayal of him lacks conviction and definition. As we read his successive wives' (and lovers') tales, we are left wondering about the source of his attractiveness to women: are they drawn to him out of the depths of self-loathing or by the hirsute appeal of his gorilla suit (Ziggy is hairy and writes "ape" books)? One of his lovers gives away the perverse secret: ". . . he has a sexist attitude towards women, which is why his face is longer and sadder, why his marriages are always breaking up. It's probably a fatal flaw in his psychological nature, a failure to be able to sustain a relationship, etc. But in the sack, he isn't a gentleman . . . . He likes sex . . . ."[75] He is the empty vessel into which unhappy women sink their desolate fantasies of redemption. By placing such a dead character at the centre of her women's lives, and by depriving the reader of any insights into his feelings and motivations, Engel forfeits the opportunity of building their stories towards some composite portrait of a beguiling "bastard."

It is not surprising that the only stories charged with deeper implications (three are placed in the third section; one is inappropriately buried in the second) together form the embryonic roots of the larger fiction that later took shape as *The Glassy Sea*. "Marshallene on Rape," "Marshallene at Work," "Ruth," and "Bicycle Story" are stories about storytelling, about the difficult art of being a sincere purveyor of family history. Here Engel returns to the emotional heartland of her novels, the vividly felt scene-settings of southwestern Ontario. This setting, and its accompanying cast of characters, she appropriated for *The Glassy Sea* and earlier drew upon in *Joanne*. These four stories, along with an experimental short fiction published elsewhere, "Atlas and Gazeteer of the West China Shore,"[76] have the extrinsic merit of revealing the genealogical roots of *The Glassy Sea*; the latter story is even subtitled "Working Notes for a Novel." Their superior quality suggests that

Engel more profitably draws upon this particular regional hoard than upon the middle-class, urban Toronto people and settings which figure in the weaker stories.

In her 1984 article "Inside the Easter Egg," Jane Rule claims that the collection "should have a more prominent place in the Engel canon than it has yet achieved."[77] Although she praises the book's "deftly shorthanded pasts and . . . richness of quickly sketched characters" (p. 42) and its funny "one-liners" and "sustained descriptions" (p. 44), Rule offers no analysis or textual evidence to support her conviction about the book's merit.

In *Bear*, Marian Engel's talent fulfils itself in an extremely fine novel, arguably her best. Her concentrated focus of vision allows her, for the first time, to get *behind* the subjective preoccupations of the early novels and to grasp directly the relationship between personal identity and the social order. As a result, *Bear* develops a far more positive and compelling vision of life than the preceding novels: its heroine seeks a rapprochement with the natural environment and, ultimately, with the realities of social experience in her search for a more clear-sighted engagement with life. Unlike Sarah and Minn, she does not take the easier route of withdrawal into the inner life by resigning herself to determinism or by oversimplifying distinctions between idealism and reality; and unlike Audrey, her individuality is not overwhelmed by her environment — it is defined by her relationship with it.

I have already outlined (see "Critical Overview and Context" above) the critical debate that followed the publication of *Bear*, and which raged around the question, Is it second-rate pornography or a mythic *tour de force*? I now suggest a consideration of the interpretive problem that firmly sets *Bear* in the primitivist tradition of such forms of myth as *Moby-Dick*, Faulkner's "The Bear," Conrad's *Heart of Darkness*, and Lawrence's *The Plumed Serpent* — and that recognizes its unique distinction of having assimilated into its recreation of a primitivist world view a *naturalistically* conceived erotic dimension. The element of double vision draws attention to the irony implicit in the critical controversy: by conducting their arguments in dualistic terms (instinctual/intellectual; erotic/rational; "dirty"/uplifting), the book's commentators entrench themselves in the very polarities Engel is struggling to reconcile.

The interlocking themes of the novel, and the primitivist context within which they are elaborated, are established in the first chapter.

Engel's selection of a quotation from Kenneth Clark's *Landscape into Art* as epigraph hints at the importance of her use of light as a symbol for the clarity of compassionate vision: "Facts become art through love, which unifies them and lifts them to a higher plane of reality; and in landscape, this all-embracing love is expressed by light." *Bear* opens with a simile for the dark, subterranean mode of existence that denies Lou's instinctual self: "In the winter, she lived like a mole, buried deep in her office, digging among maps and manuscripts."[78] When spring returned and ". . . the sun filtered into even her basement windows . . ." (p. 2), she found that ". . . her eyes would no longer focus in the light . . ." (p. 3). This lambent spring light illuminates the "flaws in her plodding private world" (p. 2) by recalling the sharply contrasting "image of the Good Life long ago stamped on her soul" (p. 3). Implicit in this contrast is the suggestion that the missing component of personality is instinctual and unconscious in nature, an unspecified revivifying power immanent in sunlight. The light/dark imagery has a natural correspondence in the phenomena of seasonal change: "In this country, . . . we have winter lives and summer lives of completely different quality" (p. 14). These subtly allusive introductory pages establish, through the imagery, the novel's basic points of reference — the disparity between the protagonist's "instinctual" and "civilized" selves. The remainder of the chapter links her search for wholeness of identity to an analogous quest for the roots of national identity. Through her bibliographical research on Cary's island, Lou hopes to uncover the suppressed side of the "Canadian tradition," thereby qualifying the prevailing academic perception of it as "genteel." The light imagery describing her scholarly aspiration echoes that of personal identity: she prays that ". . . enough would be revealed to develop the dim negative of that region's history" (p. 5). Her suggestion that the twin search for a prerational definition of identity and culture will involve a radical shedding of social preconceptions and conventions hints at the quality of moral subversiveness the novel subsequently enlarges.

Engel relies primarily on the primitivist motif to articulate her linking themes and to structure their narrative interplay in the remainder of the novel. She uses primitivism in the post-modern, conscious manner: the myth functions as a structural principle by which the concept of rites of passage organizes the narrative and determines her handling of time; as a source of metaphor which places the action in a discrete cultural/anthropological perspective;

and as a stylistic resource upon which to draw for such characteristic elements as animism, natural piety, and ritual to enrich the language of her telling.[79] *Bear* is not in the "naïve" primitivist tradition of earlier conventions of the Golden Age, the pastoral, or the Noble Savage. Engel does not urge a regression to earlier human conditions and communities; Lou herself is aware of the unreality of "thinking herself into a rugged, pastoral past that it was too late to grasp" (p. 154). The "naïve" pastoral myth, however, exerted a powerful hold on the European imagination during Colonel John Cary's day: the New World, to which he is drawn after the Peninsular Wars, represented a natural, precivilized world set against the ancient corruptions of the European consciousness. This imagined state of wilderness "innocence" was seen to be embodied in the spiritually whole aboriginal peoples, whose myths — unlike those of "civilized" man — had retained their potency. Engel consciously sets Cary's primitivist search in the literary context of the Romantic movement. She first relates his "big dream" to its historical precedents in the eighteenth-century cult of the Noble Savage by explicit references to the key texts: "Did he come entranced by the novels of Mrs. Aphra Behn, then move on to *Atala* and the idea of the noble savage, then James Fenimore Cooper?" (p. 104). As Lou reads a post-Victorian life of Beau Brummell, she reflects that "as much as Blake and Wordsworth, Cary and Brummell had wanted a better life" and "were as infected by romanticism as the poets" (p. 64). In her reading of E. J. Trelawny's biographical *Recollections of the Last Days of Shelley and Byron* (1858), she dimly perceives "some connection" between Trelawny's obsessive need to "possess" a poet and Cary's need for an island (p. 103). The Romantic longing for a new bond with the natural world is similar to Lou's own obsessive need for "some connection" with the wilderness that will release the erotic impulse buried beneath the moribund forms of contemporary civiliation.

Yet Engel is aware of the vast distance in chronology and sensibility between Cary's time and Lou's. She updates her treatment of mitivism by bringing into shocking confrontation both the sacraıtal world view central to the *idea* of the Canadian wilderness h and her protagonist's very *real* violation of a taboo central to its rvance. Her unusual strategy involves mixing two opposed ficl modes, romance and realism, as she did with far less sophisti-ı in *No Clouds of Glory*. Just as Lou is being initiated into a harmonious situation in the romantic world of primitivist myth, the process of accommodation is reversed by allowing the debased values of the real world to obtrude on the idyll.

The sacramental aspects of the primitivist myth are realized through four basic modes of ordering experience that are radically unlike Lou's "methodical" and "rational" occupational habits of mind: animism, natural piety, ritual, and the subjective experience of time. These antirational modes work allusively through the narrative to challenge, and eventually to subvert, the rational mode. Immediately upon arriving on the island, Lou senses that she is entering a process of psychic rebirth: "I have an odd sense . . . of being reborn" (p. 12). Engel establishes Lou's developing relation to the natural world by investing in her perceptions of natural phenomena an animistic spirit, which is accompanied by feelings of natural piety. Her descriptions of landscape, weather, inanimate objects — and particularly, the effect on them of light — hint at the way the wilderness and the bear will serve as Lou's bridge into the antirational. One of the many textual examples will suffice to illustrate this: "The world was furred with the late spring snow . . . . packing snow already falling in caterpillars off the greening branches . . . . She stood outside, listening. Small birds cheeped. The river sucked at reeds and stones. Branches cracked, rubbed against each other. Bird-feet rustled in dry leaves . . . . She found a break in the brush, and entered the forest solemnly, as if she were trespassing in a foreign church" (pp. 45–47; see also pp. 10, 31, 36, 40–41, 65, 108).

The third manifestation of primitivism, the investment of commonplace events with a ritualistic texture, relates to Lou's relationship with the bear. In primitive mythology, the bear lends itself to totemic uses; these are repeatedly alluded to in the series of notes about bears Lou discovers in Cary's books. Primitive man appealed to the animistic powers present in the totem through propitiatory observances (see p. 69). Lou is instructed in the proper ritualistic conduct towards the bear in an earthy, pragmatic manner under the spiritual aegis of his former keeper, an old Indian woman, who advises her: "Shit with the bear . . . . Morning, you shit, he shit. Bear lives by smell" (p. 50).

The fourth primitivist feature is the subjective apprehension of time. The primitivist consciousness is alert to those natural periodicities, such as seasonal change, that rhythmically undercut linear time. Before Lou's real initiation into the wilderness has begun, daily events are recounted in brief narrative units that "calendar" their linear progression. The novelist's handling of time then changes to signal the beginning of Lou's relationship with the bear (dramatized in the shitting ritual) to reflect the anticlock experience. Chapter viii, for example, takes the reader through an indefinite succession of days and nights during which the date and time of day remain unspecified. As the new relationship intensifies, Lou's work schedule is correspondingly undermined: the bibliographical temper gives way to the libidinal. The events of several days are tersely summarized, while episodes of brief duration that foreshadow some larger revelation (or orgasm) are expanded. Engel's use of verb tense reinforces this alternately telescopic/expansive handling of time. She consistently exploits the simple past tense to cover both habitual actions that are repeated over an extended period of time and the experience of a few unique moments (see pp. 141–43). This device has the ambiguous effect of blurring one's fixed sense of what transpires; the objective differentiations of time and space (the metronomic regularity of the rational mode) is subverted by the intuitive rhythms of the "high, whistling communion" (p. 159) that binds Lou and the bear.

The symbolic elements pertaining to the primitivist myth outlined above are strongly present in the story; however, they coexist with Lou's lived, naturalistically depicted experience of the wilderness and the bear. However accurate the commentators' descriptions of *Bear* as archetype, allegory, romance, emblem, fable, pastoral, parable, or folk tale, these descriptions are partial: Scott Symons rightly drew attention to its erotic dimension. Bear clearly has his symbolic meanings, and his story its ancient narrative roots, but he has a tangible anatomy and sexuality as well: "She cradled his big, furry, asymmetrical balls in her hands, she played with them, slipping them gently inside their cases as he licked. His prick did not come out of its long cartilaginous sheath" (pp. 129–30). If Lou's relationship with him is to function as an index both of moral stature and of the degree to which her goal of reconciling wilderness and society is attainable, then the naturalistic level must be given full play. On the level of purification rite, her relationship symbolizes only her communion of being *apart from* society. Together they exist in a state of suspension; she still must make the transition back into the "real" world that will allow the growth of moral responsibility. Engel wants to make it very clear that the problems of contemporary civilization are immeasurably more complex than those of any purely mythic wilderness. She refuses Wordsworth-style pristine epiphanies in the *head*: these moments of communion are *orgasmic* too. The intrusion of naturalistic elements into the myth forces a moral valuation of the act of bestiality. In dramatizing the primitivist alternative to the life-denying society Lou is escaping from, Engel also judges the terms in which the dramatization is enacted. Lou's eventual failure to observe the integrity of the bear's fundamental otherness represents something far more serious than a mere breach of decorum or rejection of gentility. Bestiality is a *taboo*, not a hypocritical Puritan admonition on the order of strictures against premarital sex. As a taboo object, the bear is "holy" in the sense that he brings Lou into communion with a state of innocence through her own partly instinctive, partly learned rapprochement with nature. She fails, then, to observe moral propriety on the deepest level; her exercise of sexual domination betrays this reverential bond by shifting the natural order of the relationship in favour of her own emotional and sexual imperatives. She attempts to force on the bear the selfsame rape of selfhood previously inflicted on her by men — and she knows it: "The next day she was restless, guilty. She had broken a taboo. She had changed something. The quality of her love was different now. She had gone too far with him. There was something aggressive in her that always went too far . . . . She felt empty and angry, a woman who stank of bestiality" (p. 143).

The novelist, fully capable of distinguishing between life and death, holds the moral evaluation in a tight ironic perspective. The reader is not being invited to approve of Lou's action as a victory of female selfhood; on the contrary, it is an act conceived in extreme desperation, a measure of her tragic alienation from a human(e) community. That Engel managed to bring off this delicate balance between *eros* and *agape* is a triumph of writing skill.

Lou's inability at the end of the novel to fully articulate the precise meanings of her encounter with the totemic bear (p. 162) is not an evasion on the novelist's part: to relocate her newly acquired, supra-rational wisdom on any explicit level of discourse would dissipate its meanings. However, Engel's hasty tidying-up of her heroine's quest for the Canadian identity *is* unsatisfactory; like Lou, she appears to have lost interest in the pedagogical pursuit. Whatever meaning the New World may have held for the Carys is abruptly dispensed with: "They didn't know much, people like the Carys. They were tourists

. . . . [They were] a family who did not want to be common clay, who feared more than anything being lost to history . . . . [T]he English wives had proclaimed their aristocracy among these Indian summer islands" (pp. 163–64). Engel's reversion here to the crude oversimplifications of class analysis diminishes the power of her thematic statement. "Much good it did them, [Lou] thought, perishing in the wilderness" (p. 165). Our historical memory of the "death-in-the-wilderness" reality of early Canadian settlement merits, at least, compassionate respect.

One final issue, concerned with style, rises from the critics' debate about *Bear*. Even most of its detractors praised the "lyrically simple," "strong, spare" style. Scott Symons, however, interprets the "stiltedness" of style as symptomatic of the novel's overall ruinous "pretentiousness": ". . . this 'extrinsicness' of decor and detail is more than just minor. It invades the entire prose style, as a predicate of being (or of non-being!). Because when Ms. Engel's prose leaves the 'See John run. See Mary run.' category (Ontario Methodist school primer literacy), of which 'Bear. There. Staring' is only a small example, then it becomes a kind of concerted poeticness, a few considered lines of nature-poesy . . . . These are often quite attractive in themselves, but paste-ons so far as the book is concerned as a whole."[80] Apart from indulging in the obvious rhetorical ploy of "proving" his accusation by adducing as textual evidence a *three-word* extract, Symons betrays his insensitivity to the novelist's selection of a style perfectly adapted to her subject matter and form: a deliberately simple, direct syntax; a diction marked by clarity, precise denotation, and avoidance of euphemism; a natural, colloquial tone of voice unencumbered by decoration and pomposity; in short, a virtually "transparent" style that never obtrudes on the narration by drawing attention to itself. Taken in isolation, Engel's effects run the risk of sounding as lifelessly prosaic as "primer style" because their imaginative force is cumulative.

I suggest the reader's attentive examination of the "night of the falling stars" passage that begins: "Out on the river, water-skiers buzzed like giant dragonflies" (p. 142); and concludes: "Towards dawn, the sky produced its distant, mysterious green flickering aurora" (p. 143). This beautiful and characteristic passage gives persuasive authority to those critics, like myself, who admire Engel's great strengths as a stylist. There is no pretentious stylistic inflation in these sentences. The words are simple and precise; none are needless; they deviate from their concrete referents only to allude briefly to the mythic abstractions (the "twin heroes" in the "brightness" of the galaxy) that inform the experience. Action verbs predominate, cast into the simple preterite tense. There is very little variation of sentence structure; the symmetry of the short sentences is controlled by their simple construction (generally speaking, one main clause). The rhetorical devices are few, but effective: simile, hyperbole, inversion, antithesis, repetition, and anticlimax. The three-stage spatial movement in the passage — from riverbank and upstairs library to riverbank, and then to bear's enclosure — gives a videolike effect of "still"/"scene"/"still." This varying rhythm has its temporal counterpart in the fast/slow/fast pacing of the narrative: the passage of time prior to the lovemaking is telescoped, then the brief moment of communion expands into timelessness, which is abruptly broken when Lou violates the taboo. Finally, when set in the context of the entire novel, the passage sounds resonant textual reverberations that culminate in *Bear*'s final sentence: "It was a brilliant night, all star-shine, and overhead the Great Bear and his thirty-seven thousand virgins kept her company" (p. 167).

Engel's decision to follow her book about a "bear-fucker" with one that has a cloistered nun as heroine begs for acidulous comments on their incongruence; indeed, one reviewer suggested that *The Glassy Sea* is "an act of contrition for the sensual excess of *Bear*."[81] Far from being a dramatic departure, *The Glassy Sea* simply offers a different technical orchestration of familiar themes. Like Lou, Rita Heber is a victim of the "battle of the sexes"[82] who has no anchorage in reality; her striving for certainty and a "kind of cleanness" (p. 162) leads her into high Anglican monasticism. The Eglantine order in which she spends the "happiest and most innocent" (p. 73) ten years of her life, and to which she returns as sister superior at the novel's close, is a setting analogous to the northern Ontario island to which Lou temporarily withdraws for her idiosyncratic redemption. Once more, we witness the heroine's remorseless sifting through appearances towards some surer comprehension of "the here-and-now" (p. 143), of wholeness of being not divorced from the life of society.

In the final section of *The Glassy Sea*, the narrator offers a succinct thematic summary in a metaphor that aptly describes the book's structure: "Life, I decided, is a sentence between brackets: these brackets must be seen to contain what is, not what might have been. It is useless to ponder on what might have been, but entirely proper to map the future in terms of the real past" (p. 146). The novel takes shape as a series of sentences within brackets about the protagonist's past — interpolations of experience that push against the outer limits of what they struggle to contain. The body of the narrative is a long letter addressed to Bishop Philip Yurn, in which Rita explains why she cannot accept his invitation to return as sister superior to the newly constituted Eglantine order. The monologue, her *apologia pro vita sua*, is bracketed with a framing "Prologue" and "Envoie," which flash forward to reveal her subsequent acceptance of his offer. "The Letter" itself, a long parenthetical unfolding of her life, is narrated in a different "voice": here she speaks her life as the "crazy lady from down by the sea" (p. 153). It is from within the island bracketing of time that she stills her headlong rush into madness.

Distinct disadvantages result from this type of structure. In terms of plot resolution, the encompassing frame guarantees an immediate loss of suspense: by page 11, when the reader is informed of the purpose of Rita's letter, she is already aware of the outcome of her long spiritual struggle. Perhaps Engel was gambling on the possibility of overcoming the often tedious — and warping — effect that fixed chronology can impose on a psychological novel. Yet the small frame is insufficient to mitigate the severe linearity of the letter, which comprises four-fifths of the novel. Because *The Glassy Sea* offers a sustained inner view of the protagonist, Engel's intended effects might have been better realized had she truly opened up her structure to allow for the full play of subjective time on Rita's varying mental states. As it stands, the novel is only superficially flexible in its handling of time. This is experience recollected in relative tranquility: ample time has passed "for the examination of conscience, the acquisition of tranquility in meditation" (p. 85). Because of this — and the epistolary cast in which it is set — its reflective recounting of events is unenlivened by spontaneity or surprise. The dramatic tension of irresolution is further dissipated by one's sense that Rita long ago succumbed to Lou's habit of numbing the nerve ends of experience through intellectualism.

Two themes are set in contrapuntal play within the letter's charting of the pivotal events in the heroine's life: the worldly imperatives of the erotic self and the intense drive to aestheticism of the contemplative self. Both the secular and reclusive worlds of her experience have two distinct settings: West China Township and Toronto, and the cloister and the island respectively. The West China Township of

Rita's childhood is the same ground previously trod by Sarah Porlock, Minn Burge, and Joanne. The joyless, repressive asceticism of her "ghastly Puritan background, the perfectionism" (p. 12), is once again embodied in the dour figure of the mother with her "utilitarian view of life" (p. 71). This stimulates in the adolescent a yearning for the beauty of "aesthetic forms," a beauty prefigured in the lush words of the hymn from which the novel takes its title: ". . . the golden crowns of the saints were cast in a glassy sea . . ." (p. 19). Toronto, where Rita lives during her disastrous marriage to Asher Bowen, is realized only as a mental site (cf. Minn Burge's Toronto). Her domestic life inside their "enormous house in lower Forest Hill" (p. 108) replicates her childhood experience; here she submits herself to the bloodless and life-denying asceticism of her husband, a character who is insufficiently developed to serve any function other than that of negative exemplum. Summarizing her encounters with the secular world, Rita remarks: ". . . I had failed profoundly to add anything to the quality of life. In fact, judged by any moral standards, any at all, I had soiled both the world and myself" (pp. 146–47).[83]

The two reclusive settings, the cloister and the island, offer her tranquil refuges from the world. They are connected to one another through the symbol of the rose: the rich interplay of its symbolic meanings objectifies Rita's ultimate rejection of her island sanctuary for the cloister. The cloister *is* the "rose-world" (p. 19); on the island she is only "surrounded by these roses" (p. 18). The frequent rose allusions, and all the reminiscent variations, draw one's attention to the *literal* meaning of the flower, apart from any spiritual or symbolic valuations: "*Rosa Eglanteria* is a small, five-petalled pink rose, just that" (p. 143). This exclusively nominal sense is the only one Rita is willing to accept while she is on the island. In order to see "reality" and maintain her hold on "this finally painless life" (p. 144), she must set aside the "symbolical connotations" (p. 143) that accrue to it through literary tradition and mystic experience. Acutely aware of the significance of names and naming (she frequently meditates upon the several meanings of her own religious name, Mary Pelagia), Rita cannot deny the fact that language itself is symbolic: the word "rose" *stands for* the objective flower it denotes. However, that evocation further suggests abstract meanings more compelling than its mere referent: "A rose is a woman, perhaps, but also a symbol, a flower, and the symbol of the mystery of the flower" (p. 19). This awareness culminates in an epiphany: "... for one moment I was at the heart of the roses and of the universe .... Perhaps, in that moment, I was the rose" (p. 19). As the symbol of completion, consummation, and perfection, the rose *is* the mystic Centre. The Virgin Mary, "one incarnation of the rose," represents the "stilling of time in the dead centre of the rose garden" (p. 19). The flower's resemblance to female genitalia associates it with woman's sexuality, as does Rita's religious name, Pelagia, "a false cognate of Marina who is Aphrodite" (p. 141; cf. p. 92). A symbol, then, of secular *and* devotional eroticism (Rita knows her John Donne), the rose is a finely chosen and deftly articulated symbol for the ontological poles between which Rita's divided allegiance swings. Ultimately it is the syncretic power of the rose that attracts her back to the cloister: "There is nothing uncertain about a rose, nothing tentative .... That's why I'm here. That's why I'm here" (p. 162). The contrasting meanings of the flower are subtly underpinned by Rita's repeated allusions to her own dual nature, which has its analogue in the biblical Mary-and-Martha story (see pp. 69, 139, 145, 165).

I referred earlier to the shared nexus of ideas linking *Bear* and *The Glassy Sea*; that the latter makes any thematic advance on its precursor is debatable. At the heart of the problem is the contentious issue of point of view — the unresolved ambiguity at the novel's core. As with *Bear*, reviewers voiced conflicting interpretations which leave one wondering if they have read the same book. Because he mistrusts "her ability to see straight," Dennis Duffy argued that the narrator is a naïve protagonist who is being used for ironic effect.[84] At the opposite axis of judgement, Sylvia Vance perceived no distance whatever between the norms of the narrator and those of the implied author. She advanced her heady sense of identification with this narrator/author to the extreme of endorsing a fascist program of genocide-by-gender that Rita herself, in a more lucid moment of retrospection, describes as "my mad plan for holocaust as relief" (p. 160).[85]

The most effective means of determining the degree of distance separating narrator and author — and of evaluating Engel's success in manipulating that distance in relation to her intentions — is to examine the framing device. These two sections are crucial to understanding Rita's "quest for simplifications, patterns, stylizations" (p. 65); together they should provide a controlling interpretive framework on the enclosed narrative. The endlessly shifting points of reference, the attendant prevarications and vacillations, and all the

confused pieties revealed by Rita in the "Prologue" are a sure indi-
cator that Engel is resolutely placing her narrator at a considerable
distance from herself (see pp. 9, 10, 13). That Rita sees her letter as
serving an apologetic (and therefore rhetorical) purpose does, however, confuse the issue of distance: her essentially self-defensive
rationalizations create a misleading impression that her moral vindi-
cation has considerable validity. This impression is reinforced by the
fact that her sustained inner view can have no qualifying perspective.
The most worrisome example of the danger of authorial identification with Rita comes when she vents her "mad plan for holocaust"
(pp. 146–52). Engel seems here to be speaking directly through her
narrator, thus temporarily destroying her own subtle distancing arti-
fice. This lapse from the ironic perspective markedly diminishes the
persuasive force of the book but is not fatal to clarity. Further
evidence of Rita's unreliability is provided in the "Envoie." This
concluding section is narrated by a woman who, full of "hatred and
despair" (p. 162), allows the promptings of her "black, angry,
jealous heart" (p. 152) to pervert her judgement. In addition, there is
the matter of her disingenuous and evasive tendency to simply
smother in aestheticism or sentimentalism everything that is not
reducible to empirical verification — i.e., the central tenets of belief.
As a principle of economy, it serves Rita well: she is able to commit
herself to a God in whom she has only the most tenuous belief, and to
a religious career when she has "no sure sense of vocation" (p. 159).
This trait, which severely discredits her authority, is sharply present
in her recounting of the decisive time she spent with Brother
Anthony, when her "faith" was renewed. In her conversations with
him, she poses the key obstacles to faith, the most personally compelling of which is the problem of evil (which she — and evidently the
novelist — confuses with the Manichaean doctrine of original sin,
later repudiated by the Pelagians [see p. 152]). If everything is a
manifestation of God, how can one explain the existence of her
hydrocephalic son? Rita then conveniently "forgets" Anthony's
arguments, demanding that we accept on faith their superior persua-
siveness (pp. 153–54). This refusal to address itself to the central
problem of faith, which is its raison d'être, nullifies *The Glassy Sea* as
a serious novel of ideas.

At the end of the book, the novelist, along with her heroine, gives
the impression of being *tired*: "Ah well, I guess there's nothing hypocritical in telling myself I'm starting a women's commune, and then

trying to believe in it. I don't want to lose myself in the cloud of unknowing, just to believe enough in goodness to call it God" (p. 166). In a 1981 *Globe and Mail* interview, Engel offered a candid explanation for the vacuity of her novel: "I have a tendency to go for classical lyricism. You have to be careful with that because you can end up saying nothing, but saying it very beautifully" (Corbeil, p. 3). In a later interview, she attributed her disappointment with the book to the complexity of its philosophical theme, which led her to abandon the subject before she had satisfactorily worked it through: "The whole philosophy of perfectability is an important one and I wish I had done that book better. I got so far involved in it that I would have had to spend the rest of my life on it to do it right. At the end I cut it off" (Klein, p. 30).

Engel's seventh — and final — novel, *Lunatic Villas*, exhibits a number of her distinctive narrative fingerprints. Although sounded in a new key, the dominant themes are clearly recognizable: the intersection (usually collision) of tradition and change, and its disorienting impact on personality; the vexed pursuit of female identity in the midst of fractured domesticity and culture; and the protagonist's striving for a place in a wider, more generous community that might supply what was lost in the collapse of marriage and conventional morality. The central character, Harriet Ross, shares defining personality traits with those earlier, sturdy and scrappy survivors of the inter-sex wars, Sarah Porlock, Minn Burge, Joanne, and Rita Heber. As in *No Clouds of Glory*, *The Honeyman Festival*, and *The Glassy Sea*, Toronto figures both as a setting and a symbolic locale; more specifically, Rathbone Place, the street on which the main action transpires, functions for all practical purposes as an "island" which is in some respects conceptually reminiscent of the islands that figure in *No Clouds of Glory*, *Monodromos*, *Bear*, and *The Glassy Sea*.

Yet for all these parallels with her earlier fiction, *Lunatic Villas* is a generic sport, its deviations from the Engel norm more striking than its resemblances. It stands as her only purely comedic novel, the book in which Engel took a vacation from her habitually more serious intent and gave free rein to her playful spirit, that rueful appreciation of the ludicrous that lies not far beneath the more deliberative and earnest surfaces of all her writing. She conceived of the book as an opportunity to give the feminist themes which informed *The Glassy Sea* a less polemical thrust, to make those concerns "much more implicit and understated": "I got stuck in *The Glassy*

Sea with the subject of feminism. I thought it would be a long philosophical novel, but I lost my grip on it. It didn't turn out quite the way I wanted it to."[86] Her impulse to dissolve existential complications into some summary gesture of affirmation persisted, though: "I hope *Lunatic Villas* can be described as a comic novel. Harriet and her six children are a tribute to my love of overloaded systems; and if the novel is ultimately optimistic in the face of the turmoil that the characters experience, well, it's the only position to take in a world which is so often wretched."[87] The minimalist prose style, shorn of all seductive curlicues, that she developed for the new novel was also a product of her retrospective reaction to *The Glassy Sea*: "I wanted to get out of the lush, descriptive writing I'd done before. It was beginning to drive me crazy. It was beginning to say nothing, and I wanted to say the way things really are in Toronto, not the usual pieties. So I decided to have fun with it and had a lovely time."[88]

Lunatic Villas does not convey any comprehensive sense of Toronto: its tunnel-vision focus is on the WASP residents of a few houses in one "little middle-class enclave,"[89] protectively insulated from the perilously encroaching wider community, and who are too restricted by their very limited specificity of race, class, and ethnicity to allow their chronicler to engage them in the broader issues that define the mutant culture that is cosmopolitan Toronto. One reviewer rightly complained about the dissipation of the sense of place subsequent to the "really intriguing opening."[90] The novel's true emotional heartland is located, not on the streets of Toronto, but in the protagonist's torturing memories of her early life as the abused daughter of a prematurely widowed, angry father. These memories, around which the narrative nervously circles, are given a potently extended force by the continuing intrusions into Harriet's existence of her two sisters — Babs the drunk and Madge the self-righteous shrew — who cling to their minimal survival as tattered remnants of thwarted promise. As a result of this conflicted sense of place, Harriet's excursions into the city are those of a tourist; her narrative snapshots of the "natives," particularly immigrants, remain merely quaint and stereotypic (see especially pp. 83–87).

The novel does succeed, in a more limited way, as a contemporary comedy of manners — perhaps more "renovation" than Restoration in character. Its satiric target is soft-edged, its barbs too affectionately drawn on the ultra-contemporary lifestyles of a discrete social group — the quintessentially bourgeois survivors of nuclear family fallout who take shelter in their reconstruction of, ironically, yet another garrison society. Very close to the conclusion of the novel, Harriet expresses her fears about what will happen when the wall, which has functioned throughout the story as a hermetic seal, is knocked down: "What's it going to be like when that wall is a street? she wonders. When we're connected to the rest of the city? She has seen the plans for the development many times, but this is the first day they've been real to her. They're going to let in the world, she thinks, and I may not like it" (p. 238). But "the world" has long before been given access to the city and, in its redefinition-by-possession, has expanded it far beyond Harriet's comforting hothouse environment. Harriet's inability to enlarge upon what she knows, based upon both her private terrors and her immigrant-phobia, severely diminishes Engel's thematic opportunities to examine and challenge the social relations that govern the city.

Lunatic Villas opens promisingly enough, with a brief "Prologue" that provides a potted real estate history of Rathbone Place, a cul-de-sac in "near west" Toronto (p. 8). The street, purchased in Canada's centennial year by a broker in order to occupy his wife, "consisted of a dozen houses facing each other in two rows like broken teeth, bounded on the south by a hydro substation, on the west by a mattress factory, and on the north by a neighbourhood where no one has spoken English since 1926" (p. 7). When the novel opens up from history into action in the winter of 1979, a cast of characters numerous and flaky enough to populate a sitcom has settled in. At their centre is single mother Harriet Ross and her six, sometimes seven, children (of several fathers, and not all of whom are even Harriet's progeny). Others include: Vinnie, Harriet's Thursday night lover, and his disabled, bird-breeding wife, Sylvia; political activist and soon-to-be single father Roger; Marshallene, sex activist and divorced writer (whose acquaintance the reader earlier made in *Inside the Easter Egg*); and "the people from Saskatchewan" (p. 12) whom we never meet.

The action is not so much plotted as it is allowed simply to unravel, like a multicoloured sock, into manifold complications, the groundwork for which is present in the characters' lunatic lives right from their introduction. It reads with the rushed, episodic progression of a hybrid TV program, part sitcom and part soap opera: the dialogue outweighs action, which is primarily talked about; improbable, bizarre circumstances are pushed to farcical extremes, usually accompanied by melodramatic undertones; and the characters are not developed but are allowed brief spots in which to perform their eccentric turns. While the outcome of each of the central plot dilemmas is potentially tragic, their essentially melodramatic cast — and Engel's impulse to gather it all up into a happy ending — spare the reader any serious concern with their fates.

There should be no real problem with the multiplicity of characters and subplots in *Lunatic Villas*, nor with their tidy disposal at the end: historically, these are integral components of the comic novel's baggage. I do agree, however, with those critics who expressed dissatisfaction with Engel's essentially thin portrayal of her secondary characters and her weak execution of the initially promising elements of setting. The underlying reason for these acknowledged shortcomings is the fact that the novelist had manifest difficulty in clearly defining her narrative focus. Throughout, she hovers, uncertain about where to light, between the telling of two competing stories. The textural blurring caused by her shifting attention might have been eliminated by a restructuring of the book that allowed her to realign and then integrate one tale into the other — for they *are* thematically related in significant ways. This relation — which could have imparted to the text that fine structural equipoise Engel generated in earlier books by setting in studied motion key polarities of being or desiring — gets muddled and eventually goes slack.

The story she ostensibly sets out to tell is about the construction of new modalities of family in the wake of the disintegration of the conventional family and has as its central metaphor the recovery of old neighbourhoods. Its execution is primarily comic. But the submerged story she cannot for long leave off telling, about Harriet's tormented childhood and adolescence, is a much darker one; its metaphor is cancer. I suspect that Engel was concerned that the tragic undertones of her submerged story might cut too deeply into the comic surfaces of the main story. The effect of the disjunctive tonalities of these two stories is to leave one feeling that the novelist has thrown up a bright circus tent over the site of a recent major disaster.

The comic structure — Engel's engineered marshalling of episodes through complication to resolution — is unintentionally subverted by the intrusions of the submerged story. Although the latter is allocated much less narrative space (its most notable soundings occur on pp. 25, 34, 61–69, 77, 162–64, and 188–89), its emotionally

reverberative impact is far more intense. In the mind of the protagonist, present events trigger disproportionate memories of having
been on the receiving end of male rage and violence; these memories
always trail intimations of death. Harriet fearfully reacts to her
disturbed son's angry outburst by instinctively regressing to her
younger self's surrogate-victimization by her savagely grieving father
(pp. 61–69); after witnessing the annual cancer parade, she plunges
into a profoundly depressive meditation upon death in which, again,
her father is a key player (pp. 188–89). These passages convey the
very antithesis of the Romantic spirit: this is raw, brutalizing
emotion recollected in terror.

The comic "surface" story, which concerns recovery and healing
(renovation), and the tragic "submerged" story, through which are
revealed the progressively deepening erosions of a personal history
that blights, like a terminal disease, the protagonist's restorative
mission, are in fatal collision. The resulting narrative tension is not
structurally and thematically enriching, but enervating. And the
mood of consolation and reconciliation normally attendant upon
comic resolution is not achieved at the end of this novel:

> Harriet lies in the middle of her bed, alone, raving.
> "I wanted to come to some great philosophical conclusion,"
> she says. "I wanted to win through to a slogan. But I haven't, I
> haven't." (p. 251)

She then checks her memory of a line about "hope" that has sustained her, from George Herbert's poem "The Pulley," against an old
college anthology; she discovers that "rest," *not* "hope," is "the
pulley that hauls us up to God" (p. 251). In spite of the novelist's clear
intention of pushing her book to a triumphant, unreservedly optimistic conclusion through the device of the Trans-Canada Bicycle
Race, the narrative ends on a muted note of exhaustion and lassitude.

Because she is allowed a history of family relations, Harriet, in
whose life both stories converge, is the only character in the novel's
teeming population who is developed with any real depth and complexity. This history provides the key that gives the reader sympathetic access to the thematic preoccupation with the street's construction of an unconventional family of residents linked together less by
consanguinity than by circumstance and reciprocity. Although

Harriet has functioned adequately in none of the roles allocated her within the traditional family — as daughter, sister, wife, or mother — her need for kinship persists. Like Rita Heber in *The Glassy Sea*, she strives to enlarge the contours of her shattered domestic world by building an alternative community.

Whatever its limitations, the fact that Engel, who knew at the time she was writing it that this would be her final novel, chose to funnel her observations of experience into a comic genre is a moving testament to her intellectual fortitude and her will to defiance.

She spent the last months of her life selecting, from her published (or broadcast) and unpublished short fiction, the collection of stories that make up *The Tattooed Woman*. She was assisted in this by her friend Timothy Findley, who contributed a touching Preface and whose own collection, *Dinner Along the Amazon*, had appeared the previous year in the same Penguin Short Fiction series. The collection would be much stronger had Engel or her editor excluded half-a-dozen slight pieces, most of which, in Engel's own words, "emerged from a well-disciplined Ontario subconscious that knows the ultimate virtue is in paying one's bills."[91] Yet a core of strong stories does establish something the earlier short fiction had not: Engel could write very accomplished — occasionally first-rank — short stories, several of which rise well above the mere bread-and-butter competence of her previous work in the genre.

The weak stories I have in mind include "The Last Wife," "There from Here," "Feet," "Anita's Dance," "Banana Flies," and "Two Rosemary Road, Toronto." They are unimaginatively narrated in a flat, unenergetic tone and in a workmanlike prose that lacks the graceful lyricism, gritty realism, or ribald humour which distinguishes Engel's voice when she is writing with all the stops out. Missing, too, is the apt, resonant imagery she could devise to elaborate her denser ideas — perhaps because here the thematic materials are so thin. These stories read as though they were written almost to a formula, as exemplary tales that point a moral: all feature a middle-aged, middle-class protagonist (four female, two male) who has endured failed relationships or other domestic disappointments and who, in the course of the story, makes a strong gesture in the direction of self-assertion or self-knowledge. They are uplifting, genteel, and boring — evidence of Engel writing, self-censored, for the glossy mainstream magazine market.

For having encouraged her more serious short fiction, "irrational" stories that took her in a new direction, she credits Robert Weaver, long-time producer of CBC Radio's *Anthology* program:

> For a long time I wrote short stories as practical exercises in earning necessities, chronicles to pay the bills. They did what they were told to do and failed to be any kind of art. Then irrationality decided to creep in, and the richness that comes from having written for long enough to know it is no use holding anything back. Robert Weaver . . . began to buy these irrational stories for his CBC radio program Anthology. It became easier to write them because he is the ideal reader: ready for anything but sloppy work. (p. xii)

In her Introduction, Engel goes on to distinguish between two kinds of fiction — "traditional narrative" based on "ordinary reality" (for which she claims no competence) and narrative that springs from "the irrational, the area where, when the skin of logic is pulled back, anything can happen" (p. xii). She says that the "irrational, the magical impulse," increasingly came to dominate her work (p. xiii); possibly she was influenced in this regard by the work of the Latin American writers she so much appreciated. "Super-reality," defined as "that element in everyday life where the surreal shows itself without turning French on us" (pp. xii-xiii), is the hallmark of four of the more engaging stories in this collection: "The Tattooed Woman," "Madame Hortensia, Equilibriste," "The Life of Bernard Orge," and "The Country Doctor." In freeing herself up to pursue the illogical, disquieting associations of the subconscious, Engel claimed for herself a new fictional terrain over which she could track the psychic life along the fine divide between reality and hallucination. These four stories offer fresh perspectives on familiar Engel themes: the crippling effects (particularly on the artist) of the suppression of difference within southern Ontario culture; how the unfettered imagination — creative vision — can transform our mundane perceptions of reality; and how creativity must embrace the extraordinary, albeit frightening, aspects of the seemingly banal. And Engel's choice of protagonists — two housewives, a deformed child, and a journalist — seems to suggest that this power of transformative vision does not reside exclusively in artists. Right to the end of her writing life, Engel continued to issue impassioned pleas for the licence to be unconventional in a prim, provincial society that preeminently rewards conformity.

In the title story a forty-two-year-old woman, upon discovering that her husband is having an affair with a girl half her age, develops a technique for giving her previously internalized pain and self-loathing a visible manifestation. She carves elaborate patterns into her skin: "Experience must show, she thought" (p. 6). Her obsessive acts of self-mutilation become a proud symbol of the artist's transformation of raw experience into significant visibility:

> I am an artist, now, she thought, a true artist. My body is my canvas. I am very old, and very beautiful, I am carved like an old shaman, I am an artifact of an old culture, my body is a pictograph from prehistory, it has been used and bent and violated and broken, but I have resisted. I am Somebody. (p. 8)

This keenly focused, richly detailed, and moving story is narrated by a third-person "centre of consciousness," which gives the onlooker-reader a chilling, ironically detached perspective on her morbid actions. Several reviewers (perhaps significantly, all of them male) complained that both the governing idea and its irresolution are unsatisfactory. Douglas Glover, for example, criticized "the strangely sentimental notion the reader is asked to swallow — namely that this self-pitying self-mutilation is somehow redemptive. Rather, it is a kind of hyper-romantic shorthand, the bizarre fronting for character, which reads like a wish-fulfilling fantasy . . . ."[92] They miss the subtly ironic point Engel is making through the anthropological allusions to "primitive" cultures (in the above long quotation from the text) and to "African women in the National Geographic magazine with beautiful slashes in their ebony skins" (p. 6). In our more "sophisticated," yet thoroughly misogynist, society, a woman's coming of middle age is often marked by her mate's infidelity, which can be read as the husband's perverse right of passage into rejuvenated manhood. From this explicitly feminist perspective, the emblematic significance of ritualistic scarring is thereby inverted. The dominant (male) culture perceives it as abnormal; the woman regards it merely as flesh-inscription of the psychic scarring inflicted upon her by "normal" male behaviour. Her act *is* redemptive insofar as it compels complicit others to witness what she has suffered and as it allows her to move beyond the scars of her victimization into a new condition of empowerment.

In "Madame Hortensia, Equilibriste," the narrator's bizarre nature resides in her physical being and her former celebrity: diminutive to the degree of near-dwarfdom, she overcame birth defects of an unspecified nature that made it difficult for her to learn to walk and became a famous acrobat. From her present, undistinguished vantage point as "Mrs. Robinson," resident on the outskirts of a small town where she lives contentedly with her six children in self-imposed obscurity, she spends her evenings writing her autobiography. Although she claims that hers is "not a moral story" (p. 30), she is repeatedly very explicit about the didactic motive prompting her to tell it: "The only happy people here are the ones who are ordinary" (p. 23). Madame Hortensia's story becomes a witty parable about Canadian national identity, which, Engel suggests, rests on our pinched conviction that mediocrity, if not entirely preferable to distinction, at least is in better taste! The writer engagingly alters the shape of her story to conform to her heroine's two modes of existence. Her sheltered, exquisite childhood and her exotic career are narrated as "fairy tale"; her return to "ordinary life" takes on the more prosaic contours of "Canadian fiction" (p. 25). This is a playful, inventive story.

The other two stories in this "irrational" group both play with the fantastic possibilities that open up to a woman who temporarily crosses the line separating her "ordinary life" ("The Country Doctor," p. 49) from the worlds she can inhabit imaginatively. In "The Life of Bernard Orge," Marge Elph, "middle-class and fustian and middle-aged" (p. 40), assumes a new *male* identity: with the assistance of a prosthetic caricature of a nose, she becomes "Bernard Orge, frail collector of early Rumanian icons" (p. 41). The story ends with a magic twist when her unconvincing fantasy becomes self-actualizing with the appearance of the real Bernard Orge. "The Country Doctor" is darker in mood, a Jamesian ghost story complete with a haunted Gothic house by the sea, the ghost of a dead mistress, and a mysterious widower with a face that "disintegrate[s]" (p. 60). The terrified protagonist returns at the end to "reality" and "the cynicism she had had to learn to protect herself from her imagination" (p. 49) — an option and a sanctuary not open to the writer.

An equal number of strong realistic stories in this collection undermines Engel's contention that she is "not good at traditional narrative" and that "reality brings out the worst in [her]" (p. xii). In fact, the two best stories in the book, "The Smell of Sulphur" and "Could I Have Found a Better Love Than You?," demonstrate her assured fluency in the conventions of realistic prose. The fact that this mode releases a number of characteristic narrative strengths is suggestive. Engel produced better work when she wrote from the objectifying distance afforded by third-person narration or by a first-person observer: her style is tauter and less self-engaged. These longer stories also allow her the space in which to develop those convincing eccentricities of personality that distinguish her more memorable characters, to accumulate the finely observed details of landscape and light that issue in fully realized settings, and to sound the recurrent images that so strikingly unify her materials.

"The Smell of Sulphur," a lyrical and elegiac evocation of a perfect childhood summer vacation, advances with symphonic precision in a three-part temporal progression that concludes with the simple realization that the sites and conditions of past happiness, while retrievable through memory, cannot be revisited in reality. In "Could I Have Found a Better Love Than You?" Miss Iris Terryberry, an eighty-nine-year-old flower breeder of considerable distinction and marked individuality, recounts for the narrator the story of her unconventional life. The catalogue descriptions of the floral varieties she developed correspond to central people in her life and set up lovely echoes within the narrative. Here, too, the dominant tone is elegiac: along with the death of this remarkable old woman, one senses the passing of an entire way of life in southwestern Ontario.

Two other stories deserve final mention here, because they are good and because they serve as simple elegies to the spirit of the woman who wrote them. "The Confession Tree" (which has as its epigraph *Timor Mortis Conturbat Ne*) hauntingly records another variation on the theme of retrieval of the past through memory — and of coming to a point of peaceful accord with it. The narrator, who has cancer, draws sustenance from an apple tree in her garden: "So she turned away from . . . the accounts of disease and disaster that are so reassuring to the elderly, and let the rush of Schubert in her ears pour out through her eyes into the apple tree. All the voices stopped, and there was only music and this benison of blossom" (p. 107). On a miniature scale, Engel's handling here of the recurring nature imagery is as deft and moving as it was in *Bear*. In the final story, "Gemini, Gemino," the narrator is brought to a realization that was central to Engel's own literary credo: the best fiction comes from the passionate and honest elaboration of "one's interior life" (p. 182).

Marian Engel's life and work stand as vital testimony to that conviction. And perhaps we are bound to stand in confused relation to a writer like Engel who, in the midst of her keen perception of "clouds of glory," remains ever-mindful of the deceptions the writer invites upon herself and her readers when she contrives literary "clouds" of consolation: insistently her writing tugs us back to the ground.

NOTES

¹ Doris Cowan, "The Heroine of Her Own Life," *Books in Canada*, Feb. 1978, p. 9. All further references to this work (Cowan) appear in the text.

² Carroll Klein, "A Conversation with Marian Engel," *Room of One's Own*, 9, No. 2 (June 1984), 5. All further references to this work (Klein) appear in the text.

³ Carole Corbeil, "Marian Engel: U of T Writer-in-Residence Continues to Mention the Unmentionables," *The Globe and Mail*, 14 Feb. 1981, Sec. E, p. 3. All further references to this work (Corbeil) appear in the text.

⁴ "The Girl from Glat: Memories of a Town That's Been Wiped off the Map," *Weekend Magazine*, 26 July 1975, p. 6. All further references to this work appear in the text.

⁵ Graeme Gibson, "Marian Engel," in *Eleven Canadian Novelists Interviewed by Graeme Gibson* (Toronto: House of Anansi, 1973), p. 109. All further references to this work (Gibson) appear in the text.

⁶ Aritha van Herk and Diana Palting, "Marian Engel: Beyond Kitchen Sink Realism" [interview], *Branching Out*, 5, No. 2 (1978), 40. All further references to this work (van Herk and Palting) appear in the text.

⁷ See Annette Wengle, "Marian Engel: A Select Bibliography," *Room of One's Own*, 9, No. 2 (June 1974), 96–98.

⁸ Du Barry Campau, "Women Writers Are on a Literary Cloud of Glory," *The Telegram* [Toronto], 13 Feb. 1968, p. 37.

⁹ Cathy Matyas and Jennifer Joiner, "Interpretation, Inspiration and the Irrelevant Question: Interview with Marian Engel," *University of Toronto Review*, 5 (Spring 1981), 5. All further references to this work (Matyas and Joiner) appear in the text.

¹⁰ Marian Engel, "The Woman as Storyteller," *Communiqué*, No. 8 (May 1975), p. 6. All further references to this work appear in the text.

¹¹ Phyllis Grosskurth, "A Hip, Hip and a . . . Wait, Whoa," rev. of *No*

Clouds of Glory, The Globe and Mail, 17 Feb. 1968, p. 18.

[12] Robert Fulford, "A War inside Sarah's Head," rev. of *No Clouds of Glory, Toronto Daily Star*, 6 Feb. 1968, p. 23.

[13] Grosskurth, "A Hip, Hip and a . . . Wait, Whoa," p. 18.

[14] Fulford, p. 23.

[15] Nora Sayre, "The Loss of Love," rev. of *No Clouds of Glory, The New York Times Book Review*, 25 Feb. 1968, p. 38. For positive assessments of Sarah's character, see Grosskurth and Fulford; for negative appraisals, see Sayre, and Gordon Roper, rev. of *No Clouds of Glory*, in "Letters in Canada 1968: Fiction," *University of Toronto Quarterly*, 38 (July 1969), 358–59.

[16] Grosskurth, "A Hip, Hip and a . . . Wait, Whoa," p. 18; Fulford, p. 23.

[17] Phyllis Grosskurth, "Trapped in a Biological Bathtub," rev. of *The Honeyman Festival, The Globe Magazine*, 5 Dec. 1970, p. 20.

[18] Susan Swan, "A Housewife with Mean Memories," rev. of *The Honeyman Festival, The Telegram* [Toronto], 21 Nov. 1970, p. 30.

[19] Annie Gottlieb, rev. of *The Honeyman Festival, The New York Times Book Review*, 1 Oct. 1972, p. 41.

[20] Grosskurth, "Trapped in a Biological Bathtub," p. 20.

[21] Peter Buitenhuis, "Brilliant Pastiches in Search of a Meaning," rev. of *Monodromos, The Globe and Mail*, 10 Nov. 1973, p. 32.

[22] Buitenhuis, p. 32. See also: Margaret Hogan, "South Windy," rev. of *Monodromos, Books in Canada*, Oct. 1973, pp. 9–10; Audrey Thomas, "Closing Doors," rev. of *The Book of Eve*, by Constance Beresford-Howe, and *Monodromos*, by Marian Engel, *Canadian Literature*, No. 61 (Summer 1974), pp. 80–81.

[23] Kildare Dobbs, "*Monodromos*: It's a Novel One Can Enjoy in All Ways," *The Toronto Star*, 28 Nov. 1973, Sec. G, p. 20.

[24] Ronald Blythe, "A Novel Not to Be Missed," rev. of *One Way Street, The Sunday Times* [London], 5 Jan. 1975, p. 31.

[25] Thomas, p. 81; Marni Jackson, "Novelists Roam Newfoundland, a Greek Island and Divorce World," rev. of *One Way Street* and *Joanne: The Last Days of a Modern Marriage*, by Marian Engel, and *Tomorrow Will Be Sunday*, by Harold Horwood, *The Toronto Star*, 22 Feb. 1975, Sec. F, p. 7.

[26] Sylvia Millar, "Sermons in Stone," rev. of *One Way Street, The Times Literary Supplement*, 24 Jan. 1975, p. 73.

[27] Jackson, p. 7.

[28] Elaine Feinstein, "Ghosts," rev. of *One Way Street*, by Marian Engel, *Ugetsu Monogatari*, by Ueda Akinari, *Tug of War*, by Julian Fane, and *The Last Hours before Dawn*, by Reg Gadney, *New Statesman*, 17 Jan. 1975, p. 85.

[29] Frank Davey, "Marian Engel," in *From There to Here: A Guide to English-Canadian Literature since 1960* (Erin, Ont.: Porcépic, 1974), p. 102.

[30] Myrna Kostash, "That Nice Woman Next Door," rev. of *Joanne: The Last Days of a Modern Marriage, Books in Canada*, May 1975, p. 7.

[31] Brian Vintcent, "Inside the Engel Easter Egg," *Quill & Quire*, Dec. 1975, p. 36.

[32] Roy MacSkimming, "Toughness, Affection, Humor Mark Best of Engel's Stories," rev. of *Inside the Easter Egg, The Toronto Star*, 24 Jan. 1976, Sec. H, p. 7.

[33] Ronald Labonte, rev. of *Inside the Easter Egg* and *Bear, Canadian Fiction Magazine*, Nos. 24–25 (Spring–Summer 1977), p. 185.

[34] Douglas H. Parker, "'Memories of My Own Patterns': Levels of Reality in *The Honeyman Festival*," *Journal of Canadian Fiction*, 4, No. 3 (1975), 112. All further references to this work appear in the text.

[35] Adele Wiseman, "Pooh at Puberty," rev. of *Bear, Books in Canada*, April 1976, p. 6.

[36] Elspeth Cameron, "Midsummer Madness: Marian Engel's *Bear*," *Journal of Canadian Fiction*, No. 21 (1977–78), pp. 83–94.

[37] Francis X. Jordan, rev. of *Bear, Best Sellers*, 36 (Nov. 1976), 245.

[38] Scott Symons, "The Canadian Bestiary: Ongoing Literary Depravity," *West Coast Review*, 11, No. 3 (Jan. 1977), 8.

[39] Margaret Gail Osachoff, "The Bearness of Bear," *The University of Windsor Review*, 15, Nos. 1–2 (Fall–Winter 1979 and Spring–Summer 1980), 13.

[40] Donald S. Hair, "Marian Engel's 'Bear,'" *Canadian Literature*, No. 92 (Spring 1982), p. 34. All further references to this work appear in the text.

[41] Michelle Gadpaille, "A Note on 'Bear,'" *Canadian Literature*, No. 92 (Spring 1982), pp. 151–54.

[42] Ann Hutchinson, "Marian Engel, Equilibriste," *Book Forum*, 4, No. 1 (1978), 48.

[43] Dennis Duffy, rev. of *The Glassy Sea, The Globe and Mail*, 30 Sept. 1978, p. 26.

[44] See: Sheila Robinson Fallis, rev. of *The Glassy Sea, Quill & Quire*, 8 Sept. 1978, p. 12; Duffy, p. 26; Barbara Amiel, "Bearing Up under the Strain, Part II," rev. of *The Glassy Sea, Maclean's*, 9 Oct. 1978, p. 64; Val Clery, "Look Outward, Engel, Now," rev. of *The Glassy Sea, Books in Canada*, Aug.–Sept. 1978, p. 14.

[45] See: Mary Gordon, "The Quest of Sister Mary Pelagia," rev. of *The Glassy Sea, The New York Times Book Review*, 9 Sept. 1979, pp. 12, 42;

Eleanor Wachtel, "Pleasure of Engel's Company," rev. of *The Glassy Sea*, *The Vancouver Sun*, 27 Oct. 1978, p. 40L; and Katherine Govier, "Patching Up the Victims," rev. of *The Glassy Sea*, *The Canadian Forum*, March 1979, p. 30.

[46] Ken Adachi, "Engel Follows *Bear* with a Novel of Uneven Riches," rev. of *The Glassy Sea*, *The Toronto Star*, 30 Sept. 1978, Sec. D, p. 7.

[47] Alan Twigg, "Private Eye: Marian Engel," in *For Openers: Conversations with Twenty-Four Canadian Writers* (Madeira Park, B.C.: Harbour, 1981), pp. 197–205.

[48] George Woodcock, "Casting Down Their Golden Crowns: Notes on *The Glassy Sea*," *Room of One's Own*, 9, No. 2 (June 1984), 46–53. All further references to this work appear in the text.

[49] See, for example: Ken Adachi, "Absurd and Absorbing Novel from Marian Engel," rev. of *Lunatic Villas*, *The Toronto Star*, 7 March 1981, Sec. F, p. 10; Helen Hoy, rev. of *Lunatic Villas*, in "Letters in Canada 1981: Fiction," *University of Toronto Quarterly*, 51 (Summer 1982), 329–30; Barbara Amiel, "Insight, with a High Price of Admission," rev. of *Lunatic Villas*, *Maclean's*, 9 March 1981, p. 62; Beth Greenwood, rev. of *Lunatic Villas*, *Quarry*, 31, No. 1 (Winter 1982), 96–97; and Doris Cowan, "A Fine Madness," rev. of *Lunatic Villas*, *Books in Canada*, April 1981, pp. 20–21.

[50] See: Hoy, p. 329; Greenwood, p. 96; Cowan, "A Fine Madness," p. 21; and William French, rev. of *Lunatic Villas*, *The Globe and Mail*, 7 March 1981, Sec. E, p. 16.

[51] Adachi, "Absurd and Absorbing Novel from Marian Engel," p. 10.

[52] Greenwood, p. 97.

[53] For positive assessments of the secondary characters, see Adachi, "Absurd and Absorbing Novel from Marian Engel," p. 10, and Hoy, p. 330; negative comments are taken from: Urjo Kareda, "Children and Chaos," rev. of *Lunatic Villas*, *Saturday Night*, May 1981, p. 56; Greenwood, p. 96; and French, p. 16, respectively.

[54] See Cowan, "A Fine Madness," p. 20, and Greenwood, p. 97, respectively.

[55] Cowan, "A Fine Madness," pp. 20–21, and Kareda, p. 56.

[56] Adachi, "Absurd and Absorbing Novel from Marian Engel," p. 10, and Anne Collins, "On the Racks," rev. of *Lunatic Villas*, by Marian Engel, and five other books, *Books in Canada*, March 1982, p. 28.

[57] John Bemrose, "A Graceful Epitaph," rev. of *The Tattooed Woman*, *Maclean's*, 5 Aug. 1985, p. 51.

[58] Patricia Morley, "Superb Last Stories Match Best Engel Novels," rev. of *The Tattooed Woman*, *The Citizen* [Ottawa], 20 July 1985, Sec. C, p. 2.

[59] Gerald Hill, "Dazzling Book by Simply Great Writer," rev. of *The Tattooed Woman*, *The Calgary Herald*, 25 Aug. 1985, Sec. C, p. 8.

[60] Douglas Glover, "Bodily Harm," rev. of *The Tattooed Woman*, *Books in Canada*, Aug.–Sept. 1985, p. 15.

[61] Ken Adachi, "In Need of a Bigger Canvas," rev. of *The Tattooed Woman*, *The Toronto Star*, 20 July 1985, Sec. M, p. 5.

[62] *No Clouds of Glory* (Don Mills, Ont.: Longmans, 1968), p. 4. Further references to this work appear in the text.

[63] *No Clouds of Glory* was reprinted in paperback as *Sarah Bastard's Notebook* (Don Mills, Ont.: Paperjacks, 1974).

[64] See especially Chapters ix and xii in their entirety, and the extended passages on pp. 69–74, 79–81, 88–94, 135–36, 177–78.

[65] See esp. pp. 11, 31, 49, 80, 88, 101, 120, 172.

[66] See esp. pp. 11, 22, 41, 48, 119, 169, 172.

[67] *The Honeyman Festival* (Toronto: House of Anansi, 1970), p. 15. All further references to this work appear in the text.

[68] Minn's visit by the social worker in Chapter ii is strikingly reminiscent of a scene in Truffaut's *The 400 Blows*: the *cinéma vérité* interview between Antoine, the protagonist (like Minn, a misfit who is stifled by conventional social definitions), and a prying social worker.

[69] See: Grosskurth, "Trapped in a Biological Bathtub," p. 20; Gottlieb, p. 40; and Davey, pp. 100–101.

[70] *Monodromos* (Toronto: House of Anansi, 1973), p. 179. All further references to this work appear in the text.

[71] See, for example: James Joyce, *Ulysses*; Virginia Woolf, *Mrs. Dalloway*; Lawrence Durrell, *The Alexandria Quartet*; William Faulkner, *The Sound and the Fury* and *As I Lay Dying*; Sheila Watson, *The Double Hook*; Graeme Gibson, *Five Legs* and *Communion*; Jane Rule, *Contract with the World*.

[72] William Butler Yeats, "Sailing to Byzantium," in *Collected Poems of W. B. Yeats* (London: Macmillan, 1963), p. 217.

[73] Marian Engel, Preface, *Joanne: The Last Days of a Modern Marriage* (Don Mills, Ont.: Paperjacks, 1975), n. pag. All further references to this work appear in the text.

[74] "The Salt Mines," in *Inside the Easter Egg* (Toronto: House of Anansi, 1975), p. 34.

[75] "Marshallene on Rape," in *Inside the Easter Egg*, p. 107.

[76] Marian Engel, "Atlas and Gazeteer of the West China Shore: Working Notes for a Novel," *Queen's Quarterly*, 82 (Spring 1975), 92–95.

[77] Jane Rule, "Inside the Easter Egg," *Room of One's Own*, 9, No. 2

(June 1984), p. 41.

[78] *Bear* (1976; rpt. Toronto: Seal, 1977), p. 1. All further references to this work appear in the text.

[79] I am deeply indebted throughout this discussion of primitivism to Michael Bell's excellent monograph, *Primitivism*, The Critical Idiom, No. 20 (London: Methuen, 1972).

[80] Symons, p. 7.

[81] Clery, p. 14.

[82] *The Glassy Sea* (Toronto: McClelland and Stewart, 1978), p. 161. All further references to this work appear in the text.

[83] In the Seal Books paperback edition (1979) of *The Glassy Sea*, the phrase "equality of life" (which appears on p. 146 of the McClelland and Stewart edition) has been emended to read "quality of life" (p. 143). In my quotation, I have used the Seal Books version.

[84] Duffy, p. 26.

[85] Sylvia Vance, "A Novel Worth the Wait," rev. of *The Glassy Sea*, *Branching Out*, 6, No. 1 (1979), 52.

[86] Ken Adachi, "The Versatility of Marian Engel," *The Toronto Star*, 8 March 1981, Sec. D, p. 12.

[87] Adachi, "The Versatility of Marian Engel," p. 12.

[88] Michael Ryval, "A Satiric Engel on Toronto Society," *Quill & Quire*, March 1981, p. 60.

[89] *Lunatic Villas* (Toronto: McClelland and Stewart, 1981), p. 239. All further references to this work appear in the text.

[90] Greenwood, p. 97.

[91] Introd., *The Tattooed Woman* (Markham, Ont.: Penguin, 1985), p. xiii. All further references to this work appear in the text.

[92] Glover, p. 15.

SELECTED BIBLIOGRAPHY

For a comprehensive bibliography of Marian Engel, the reader is referred to Annette Wengle's excellent, unpublished work, "Marian Engel: An Annotated Bibliography" (University of Toronto, Faculty of Library Science, 1979). It lists most of the known published primary and secondary writings, as well as "Audio-Visual Resources" (based on the CBC Archives card catalogue). Annette Wengle's "Marian Engel: A Selected Bibliography" (see below) provides a selection of Engel's published writings current to Spring 1984; secondary sources are not included. Wengle's complete bibliography will be published in *The Annotated Bibliography of Canada's Major Authors*, ed. Robert Lecker and Jack David, Vol. VII (in press). In March 1983, Marian Engel presented her papers to the Mills Memorial Library of McMaster University. The collection includes all the extant manuscripts of her published and unpublished writings, as well as some correspondence and her notebooks. For a complete listing, see *The Marian Engel Archive*, compiled by Dr. K. E. Garay with the assistance of Norma Smith, *Library Research News* [McMaster Univ.], 8, No. 2 (Fall 1984).

Primary Sources

Books

Engel, Marian. *No Clouds of Glory*. Don Mills, Ont.: Longmans, 1968. Rpt. *Sarah Bastard's Notebook*. Don Mills, Ont.: Paperjacks, 1974.

————. *The Honeyman Festival*. Toronto: House of Anansi, 1970.

————. *Monodromos*. Toronto: House of Anansi, 1973. Rpt. *One Way Street*. Don Mills, Ont.: Paperjacks, 1974.

————. *Adventure at Moon Bay Towers*. Toronto: Clarke, Irwin, 1974.

————. *Inside the Easter Egg*. Anansi Fiction, No. 35. Toronto: House of Anansi, 1975.

————. *Joanne: The Last Days of a Modern Marriage*. Don Mills, Ont.: Paperjacks, 1975.

———. *Bear.* 1976; rpt. Toronto: Seal, 1977.

———. *My Name Is Not Odessa Yarker.* Toronto: Kids Can, 1977.

———. *The Glassy Sea.* Toronto: McClelland and Stewart, 1978.

———, and J. A. Kraulis. *The Islands of Canada.* Edmonton: Hurtig, 1981.

———. *Lunatic Villas.* Toronto: McClelland and Stewart, 1981.

———. *The Tattooed Woman.* Markham, Ont.: Penguin, 1985.

Contributions to Periodicals

Engel, Marian. "Atlas and Gazeteer of the West China Shore: Working Notes for a Novel." *Queen's Quarterly,* 82 (Spring 1975), 92–95.

———. "The Woman as Storyteller." *Communiqué,* No. 8 (May 1975), pp. 6–7, 44–45.

———. "The Girl from Glat: Memories of a Town That's Been Wiped off the Map." *Weekend Magazine,* 26 July 1975, pp. 6–7.

Secondary Sources

Adachi, Ken. "Engel Follows *Bear* with Unsettling Novel of Uneven Riches." Rev. of *The Glassy Sea. The Toronto Star,* 30 Sept. 1978, Sec. D, p. 7.

———. "Absurd and Absorbing Novel from Marian Engel." Rev. of *Lunatic Villas. The Toronto Star,* 7 March 1981, Sec. F, p. 10.

———. "The Versatility of Marian Engel." *The Toronto Star,* 8 March 1981, Sec. D, p. 12.

———. "In Need of a Bigger Canvas." Rev. of *The Tattooed Woman. The Toronto Star,* 20 July 1985, Sec. M, p. 5.

Amiel, Barbara. "Bearing Up under the Strain, Part II." Rev. of *The Glassy Sea. Maclean's,* 9 Oct. 1978, p. 64.

———. "Insight, with a High Price of Admission." Rev. of *Lunatic Villas. Maclean's,* 9 March 1981, p. 62.

Bell, Michael. *Primitivism.* The Critical Idiom, No. 20. London: Methuen, 1972.

Bemrose, John. "A Graceful Epitaph." Rev. of *The Tattooed Woman. Maclean's,* 5 Aug. 1985, p. 51.

Blythe, Ronald. "A Novel Not to Be Missed." Rev. of *One Way Street. The Sunday Times* [London], 5 Jan. 1975, p. 31.

Buitenhuis, Peter. "Brilliant Pastiches in Search of a Meaning." Rev. of *Monodromos*. *The Globe and Mail*, 10 Nov. 1973, p. 32.

Cameron, Elspeth. "Midsummer Madness: Marian Engel's *Bear*." *Journal of Canadian Fiction*, No. 21 (1977–78), pp. 83–94.

Campau, Du Barry. "Women Writers Are on a Literary Cloud of Glory." *The Telegram* [Toronto], 13 Feb. 1968, p. 37.

Clery, Val. "Look Outward, Engel, Now." Rev. of *The Glassy Sea*. *Books in Canada*, Aug.–Sept. 1978, p. 14.

Collins, Anne. "On the Racks." Rev. of *Lunatic Villas*, by Marian Engel, and five other books. *Books in Canada*, March 1982, pp. 27–29.

Corbeil, Carole. "Marian Engel: U of T Writer-in-Residence Continues to Mention the Unmentionables." *The Globe and Mail*, 14 Feb. 1981, Sec. E, p. 3.

Cowan, Doris. "The Heroine of Her Own Life." *Books in Canada*, Feb. 1978, pp. 7–10.

———. "A Fine Madness." Rev. of *Lunatic Villas*. *Books in Canada*, April 1981, pp. 20–21.

Davey, Frank. "Marian Engel." In *From There to Here: A Guide to English-Canadian Literature since 1960*. Erin, Ont.: Porcépic, 1974, pp. 99–100, 102.

Dobbs, Kildare. "*Monodromos*: It's a Novel One Can Enjoy in All Ways." *The Toronto Star*, 28 Nov. 1973, Sec. G, p. 20.

Duffy, Dennis. Rev. of *The Glassy Sea*. *The Globe and Mail*, 30 Sept. 1978, p. 26.

Fallis, Sheila Robinson. Rev. of *The Glassy Sea*. *Quill & Quire*, 8 Sept. 1978, p. 12.

Feinstein, Elaine. "Ghosts." Rev. of *One Way Street*, by Marian Engel, *Ugetsu Monogatari*, by Ueda Akinari, *Tug of War*, by Julian Fane, and *The Last Hours before Dawn*, by Reg Gadney. *New Statesman*, 17 Jan. 1975, p. 85.

French, William. Rev. of *Lunatic Villas*. *The Globe and Mail*, 7 March 1981, Sec. E, p. 16.

Fulford, Robert. "A War inside Sarah's Head." Rev. of *No Clouds of Glory*. *Toronto Daily Star*, 6 Feb. 1968, p. 23.

Gadpaille, Michelle. "A Note on 'Bear.'" *Canadian Literature*, No. 92 (Spring 1982), pp. 151–54.

Gibson, Graeme. "Marian Engel." In *Eleven Canadian Novelists Interviewed by Graeme Gibson*. Toronto: House of Anansi, 1973, pp. 85–114.

Glover, Douglas. "Bodily Harm." Rev. of *The Tattooed Woman*. *Books in Canada*, Aug.–Sept. 1985, p. 15.

Gordon, Mary. "The Quest of Sister Mary Pelagia." Rev. of *The Glassy Sea*. *The New York Times Book Review*, 9 Sept. 1979, pp. 12, 42.

Gottlieb, Annie. Rev. of *The Honeyman Festival*. *The New York Times Book Review*, 1 Oct. 1972, pp. 40–41.

Govier, Katherine. "Patching Up the Victims." Rev. of *The Glassy Sea*. *The Canadian Forum*, March 1979, p. 30.

Greenwood, Beth. Rev. of *Lunatic Villas*. *Quarry*, 31, No. 1 (Winter 1982), 96–97.

Grosskurth, Phyllis. "A Hip, Hip and a . . . Wait, Whoa." Rev. of *No Clouds of Glory*. *The Globe Magazine*, 17 Feb. 1968, p. 18.

———. "Trapped in a Biological Bathtub." Rev. of *The Honeyman Festival*. *The Globe Magazine*, 5 Dec. 1970, p. 20.

Hair, Donald S. "Marian Engel's 'Bear.'" *Canadian Literature*, No. 92 (Spring 1982), pp. 34–45.

Hill, Gerald. "Dazzling Book by Simply Great Writer." Rev. of *The Tattooed Woman*. *The Calgary Herald*, 25 Aug. 1985, Sec. C, p. 8.

Hogan, Margaret. "South Windy." Rev. of *Monodromos*. *Books in Canada*, Oct. 1973, pp. 9–10.

Hoy, Helen. Rev. of *Lunatic Villas*. In "Letters in Canada 1981: Fiction." *University of Toronto Quarterly*, 51 (Summer 1982), 329–30.

Hutchinson, Ann. "Marian Engel, Equilibriste." *Book Forum*, 4, No. 1 (1978), 46–55.

Jackson, Marni. "Novelists Roam Newfoundland, a Greek Island and Divorce World." Rev. of *One Way Street* and *Joanne: The Last Days of a Modern Marriage*, by Marian Engel, and *Tomorrow Will Be Sunday*, by Harold Horwood. *The Toronto Star*, 22 Feb. 1975, Sec. F, p. 7.

Jordan, Francis X. Rev. of *Bear*. *Best Sellers*, 36 (Nov. 1976), 245.

Kareda, Urjo. "Children and Chaos." Rev. of *Lunatic Villas*. *Saturday Night*, May 1981, p. 56.

Klein, Carroll. "A Conversation with Marian Engel." *Room of One's Own*, 9, No. 2 (June 1984), 5–30.

Kostash, Myrna. "That Nice Woman Next Door." Rev. of *Joanne: The Last Days of a Modern Marriage*. *Books in Canada*, May 1975, pp. 6–8.

Labonte, Ronald. Rev. of *Inside the Easter Egg* and *Bear*. *Canadian Fiction Magazine*, Nos. 24–25 (Spring–Summer 1977), pp. 183–90.

MacSkimming, Roy. "Toughness, Affection, Humor Mark Best of Engel's Stories." Rev. of *Inside the Easter Egg*. *The Toronto Star*, 24 Jan. 1976, Sec. H, p. 7.

Matyas, Cathy, and Jennifer Joiner. "Interpretation, Inspiration and the Irrelevant Question: Interview with Marian Engel." *University of*

Toronto Review, 5 (Spring 1981), 4–8.

Millar, Sylvia. "Sermons in Stone." Rev. of *One Way Street*. *The Times Literary Supplement*, 24 Jan. 1975, p. 73.

Morley, Patricia. "Superb Last Stories Match Best Engel Novels." Rev. of *The Tattooed Woman*. *The Citizen* [Ottawa], 20 July 1985, Sec. C, p. 2.

Osachoff, Margaret Gail. "The Bearness of Bear." *The University of Windsor Review*, 15, Nos. 1–2 (Fall–Winter 1979 and Spring–Summer 1980), 13–21.

Parker, Douglas H. "'Memories of My Own Patterns': Levels of Reality in *The Honeyman Festival*." *Journal of Canadian Fiction*, 4, No. 3 (1975), 111–16.

Roper, Gordon. Rev. of *No Clouds of Glory*. In "Letters in Canada 1968: Fiction." *University of Toronto Quarterly*, 38 (July 1969), 358–59.

Rule, Jane. "Inside the Easter Egg." *Room of One's Own*, 9, No. 2 (June 1984), 41–45.

Ryval, Michael. "A Satiric Engel on Toronto Society." *Quill & Quire*, March 1981, p. 60.

Sayre, Nora. "The Loss of Love." Rev. of *No Clouds of Glory*. *The New York Times Book Review*, 25 Feb. 1968, pp. 38–39.

Swan, Susan. "A Housewife with Mean Memories." Rev. of *The Honeyman Festival*. *The Telegram* [Toronto], 21 Nov. 1970, p. 30.

Symons, Scott. "The Canadian Bestiary: Ongoing Literary Depravity." *West Coast Review*, 11, No. 3 (Jan. 1977), 3–16.

Thomas, Audrey. "Closing Doors." Rev. of *The Book of Eve*, by Constance Beresford-Howe, and *Monodromos*, by Marian Engel. *Canadian Literature*, No. 61 (Summer 1974), pp. 79–81.

Twigg, Alan. "Marian Engel: Private Eye." In *For Openers: Conversations with Twenty-Four Canadian Writers*. Madeira Park, B.C.: Harbour, 1981, pp. 197–205.

Vance, Sylvia. "A Novel Worth the Wait." Rev. of *The Glassy Sea*. *Branching Out*, 6, No. 1 (1979), 52.

van Herk, Aritha, and Diana Palting. "Marian Engel: Beyond Kitchen Sink Realism" [interview]. *Branching Out*, 5, No. 2 (1978), 12–13, 40.

Vintcent, Brian. "Inside the Engel Easter Egg." Rev. of *Inside the Easter Egg*. *Quill & Quire*, Dec. 1975, pp. 29, 36.

Wachtel, Eleanor. "Pleasure of Engel's Company." Rev. of *The Glassy Sea*. *The Vancouver Sun*, 27 Oct. 1978, p. 40L.

Wengle, Annette. "Marian Engel: A Select Bibliography." *Room of One's Own*, 9, No. 2 (June 1984), 92–99.

Wiseman, Adele. "Pooh at Puberty." Rev. of *Bear*. *Books in Canada*, April

1976, pp. 6–8.

Woodcock, George. "Casting Down Their Golden Crowns: Notes on *The Glassy Sea*." *Room of One's Own*, 9, No. 2 (June 1984), 46–53.